Rosie, Mary

Everyman's Poetry
Everyman, I will go with thee,
and be thy guide

Talking of Mothers
Poems for Every Mother   r

father

Selected and edited by
DOUGLAS BROOKS-DAVIES

My love always to all
three of you. Markley.

+ + +

EVERYMAN
J.M. Dent · London

This edition first published by Everyman Paperbacks in 2001
Selection, introduction and other critical apparatus
© J.M. Dent 2001

J.M. Dent
Orion Publishing Group
Orion House
5 Upper Saint Martin's Lane
London WC2H 9EA

Typeset by Set Systems Ltd, Saffron Walden, Essex
Printed in Great Britain by
The Guernsey Press Co Ltd, Guernsey, C.I.

British Library Cataloguing-in-Publication
Data is available on request

ISBN: 0 460 88223 6

Contents

Note on the Editor

Douglas Brooks-Davies was born in Wimbledon in 1942 and educated at Merchant Taylors' School, Crosby, and Brasenose College, Oxford. He was Senior Lecturer in English Literature at the University of Manchester English Department until 1993, and is now an Honorary Research Fellow there. His hobbies are gardening, singing and playing the oboe.

His books include *Number and Pattern in the Eighteenth-Century Novel* (Routledge, 1973), *The Mercurian Monarch* (Manchester U. P., 1983), *Pope's 'Dunciad' and the Queen of Night* (Manchester U. P., 1985) and *Oedipal Hamlet* (Macmillan, 1989). Among his editions are *Silver Poets of the Sixteenth Century* (Dent, 1992), *Spenser: Selected Shorter Poems* (Longman, 1995), *Spenser's 'Fairy Queen'* (Dent, 1996), L.P. Hartley's *The Go-Between* (Penguin, 1997), and Henry Fielding's *Tom Jones* and Charlotte Brontë's *Jane Eyre* (both Dent, 1998). His previous volumes for Everyman Poetry Library are *Alexander Pope* (1996), *Robert Herrick* (1996), *Four Metaphysical Poets* (1997), *Jane Austen* (1998), *Sweet Will Be The Flower: Poems on Gardens* (1999) and *What Sweeter Music: Poems on Music* (2000).

Introduction

Just as, in western tradition, music begins with the fabled Greek harpist Orpheus, and the origin of gardens is rooted in the Garden of Eden, so mothers, too, emerge out of myth: Eve, Ceres (known as Demeter to the Greeks), Niobe and (the point where myth becomes history) the Virgin Mary. Some poems in this anthology are explicitly about these mothers. Others acknowledge their mythological and cultural background much less directly. For example, Robert Herrick's little poem 'To Dianeme. A Ceremony in Gloucester' (first published in 1648 and printed here) contains, according to the *Oxford English Dictionary*, the first mention of 'Mothering', or Mother's Day, and of its customary accompanying gift, the rich fruit cake known as simnel. Behind Herrick's poem, however, lies a long and ancient tradition stretching back at least as far as ancient Rome. As the antiquarian William Hone explained in his *The Every-Day Book; or, Everlasting Calendar of Popular Amusements* (1826), under the heading Mid-Lent Sunday or Mothering Sunday:

> It is still a custom on Mid-Lent Sunday in many parts of England, for servants and apprentices to carry cakes or some nice eatables or trinkets, as presents to their parents; and in other parts, to visit their mother for a meal of furmity [frumenty, or wheat cooked in milk and seasoned with cinnamon and sugar], or to receive cakes from her with a blessing. This is called going a-mothering.

Hone goes on to explain that 'going a-mothering is from the Roman Catholic custom of going to the mother-church on Mid-Lent Sunday, to make offerings at the high altar; and that custom of the Romish Church is derived from the Hilaria' (p. 359).

The Hilaria celebrated Cybele, the earth mother and reputed mother of the gods, on 25 March annually; so that at the root of more modern feasts of mothering lies a myth of our origins with mother earth and, as Hone reminds us, the image of mother church, as in Galatians 4, and 1 Peter 2:2, with its reference to the maternal milk of the divine word.

The appropriation of pagan practice by Christianity – so that here mother earth becomes mother church – is a common one; so, too, the slippage from mother church to ordinary child-bearing woman is an instance of the familiar process by which things once the province of the divine become secularised. Thomas Hardy comments on it in *Tess of the D'Urbervilles* (1891), when he observes that the May walk of local women is a solitary remnant of an ancient, now unrecognised, Cerealia (chapter 2).

Similarly, few of us are aware, as we give our flowers and floral cards on Mother's Day, of the link between our own maternal spring festival and seed-nourishing and flower-producing mother earth, who in one form was indeed the Cybele of the Hilaria, but in another was Ceres, the goddess of flowers and grain (cereals). She was Cybele's daughter, and her Greek name Demeter was long misunderstood as meaning earth-mother. Ceres-Demeter's own daughter (Proserpina in Latin, Persephone in Greek) was abducted by the god of the underworld while gathering flowers. According to the myth, after much searching and heartache on Ceres' part, she was restored to her grieving mother for half the year, during which time vegetation flourishes. When she returns to the underworld, Ceres' grieving begins again, and the earth is covered in winter gloom and desolation. It is no accident that a meal of wheat-based frumenty, that dish of Ceres, was traditional on Mothering Sunday, according to Hone and others.

Ceres-Demeter appears in this volume in an extract from Tennyson's *Demeter and Persephone* (1889), for Tennyson, that supreme poet of melancholy and bereavement, evokes the level of grieving maternal desolation almost better than anyone. His poem balances the extract from Arthur Golding's translation of the Roman poet Ovid's *Metamorphoses* concerning Niobe, punished for her pride in her children by being transformed into permanently weeping stone. Published three centuries earlier than Tennyson's version of an equally old story, Golding's allegory of the sheer numbness of maternal heartbreak complements Demeter's sense of loss while withholding any hope of the return of even one of her offspring: like the end of Shakespeare's *King Lear*, all remains 'cheerless, dark, and deadly'.

It may be thought perverse to start an introduction to an anthology of poems on mothers and motherhood with evocations of such gloom. Yet a reading of the poems themselves will be enough to show how far our sentimental image of motherhood, compounded as it is by the Patience Strong kind of verse that inhabits the cards we buy each March, is from the experience of earlier centuries. Some women bear children easily. Others, because of physical or financial circumstances, still don't. These latter will recognise the emotions registered in many of the poems printed here: fear of childbirth, fear of perinatal mortality (both infant and maternal), the failure in the end of the father fully to engage with mother and child, and so on.

So, many readers will perhaps be shocked by the number of poems about infant death. Yet this was the statistical reality for so many that it was actually the norm in western Europe until very recently. Forget the privileges of medicine in its modern phase, and we are back with the world that begot the tale of Niobe – a world where the gods are cruel and punish you by stealing the lives of your young ones, and in which no vegetation myth offers the comfort of cyclical restoration.

Even if we change our perspective slightly and look at the first poems in this anthology with their explicitly Christian content, we find that they, too, are aware of loss: celebrating the infant Jesus and the motherhood of Mary as they do, they too know that motherhood and grief are inseparable. The baby will die as a young middle-aged man to repair the ravages wrought by that Hebraeo-Christian archetypal mother Eve who, according to the book of Genesis, brought death into the world. Mary's lullabies become elegies while Herod rages around outside, ordering boy babies to be slaughtered by the hundred; and as she nurses her baby, Mary anticipates the role she will assume in taking Christ from the cross, bearing his adult body as she bore his infant one.

Indeed, it is almost impossible to find a poem about mothers in the eighteenth century that isn't an elegy for a dead infant: here more than ever before it becomes apparent that elegy is a generic complement to lullaby. Though there are, of course, exceptions: Mary Barber's fond piece on her son first putting on breeches, Ambrose Philips's poem 'To Miss Charlotte Pulteney in Her Mother's Arms, 1 May 1724' (where the precision of the dating

makes it as precious and particular as a photograph), Mrs
Barbauld on 'Washing Day', and, perhaps best of all, Ann
Yearsley siding with mothers against nurses on the bringing up
of children.

How perennial that battle is! We find it again in Locker-
Lampson's wicked little piece ('A Terrible Infant'), Elizabeth
Barrett Browning's 'Isobel's Child', where mother takes over the
night care while the nurse sleeps, and Edith Nesbit's well-known
'Song' ('Oh, baby, baby, baby dear'), with its moment of private
maternal tenderness stolen from the world of the nanny and the
nursery. These poems are, in their various ways, as refreshing as
Francis Quarles's 'On the Infancy of Our Saviour' with its sudden
glimpses of real family life as it imagines the baby 'perking' on
Mary's knee, nuzzling her breast, glimpses his 'desperate eyes'
and imagines him, as his legs gain strength, 'diddl[ing] up and
down the room'.

So many of these poems register tenderness, and so many of
them pain. This is, I think, as it should be. Illegitimacy was a
real social problem until very recently (and often still remains
so); child death was inescapable; hard labour was the reality of
life for the majority of women. As we read on in this anthology,
we hear women speaking increasingly for themselves: about the
loss of the maiden (maternal) name (Jane Cave); about unmarried
mothers being driven to murder (Helen Leigh); about the pain of
having to earn a living knowing that your illegitimate daughter
is being brought up elsewhere (Ellen Johnston); about the death
of mother and child in (male-engineered) war (Lilian Bowes
Lyon); about the difficulty of summoning up maternal feelings
(Alice Meynell, 'The Modern Mother').

But we also hear men: Stevenson, more attached to nanny
than to mummy ('To Alison Cunningham From Her Boy'); Praed
on his dead mother; John Masefield on his dead mother, and the
impossibility of ever repaying the pain and anxiety we have
caused in our birth and upbringing; Coventry Patmore struggling
to become a good and loving father with his wife dead and his
son desperately missing her.

The anthology finishes with a poem by Elizabeth Jennings, 'To
My Mother at 73'. If we don't already identify with it, most of us
will at some stage of our lives: mutual need; the fear of hurting;
the resentment at not being allowed to grow up (and the guilt

consequent upon that resentment); the love underlying the whole relationship; and – that freighted word – the duty, too:

> Can you sense the tears
> So pent up, so afraid of hurting you?
> Must we both fumble not to show our fears
> Of holding back our pain, our kindness too?

DOUGLAS BROOKS-DAVIES

Note on the Texts

Where necessary, I have given sources for texts used in the Notes. Spelling and punctuation have been modernised, except in the case of works written over the past century or so. Titles in square brackets are editorial.

Talking of Mothers

JOHN AUDELAY

'The Mother of Mary'

The mother of Mary, that merciful may,
  Pray for us both night and day.

Sweet Saint Anne, we thee beseech
  Thou pray for us to Our Lady
That she will be our soulès leech   5
  That day when we shall die;
    Herefore we say:

Through thee was gladded all this world
  When Mary of thee bornè was,
That bore that bairn, that blissful Lord   10
  That grants us all mercy and grace;
    Herefore we say:

Barren thou wert full long before;
  Then God He say to thy meekness
That thou shouldest deliver that was forlore: 15
  Man's soul, that lay in fiendish distress;
    Herefore we say:

Fore Joachim, that holy husband,
  Prayed to God full patiently
That He would send his sweet son,   20
  Some fruit between you two to be;
    Herefore we say:

Then God He granted graciously
  Between you two a flower should spring;
The root thereof is cleped Jesse,   25
  That joy and bliss to the world shall bring;
    Herefore I say:

The blissful branch this flower on grew
   Out of Jesse, at my weeting,
Was Mary mild, that bare Jesu,
   Maiden and mother to heaven King;   30
      Herefore I say:

Ycalled Jesu of Nazareth,
   God's Son of high degree,
As here as man that suffered death   35
   And reigned into David dignity;
      Herefore I say:

In Bethlem, in that blessed place,
   Mary mild this flower hath born,
Between an ox and an ass,
   To save his people that was forlorn;   40
      Herefore I say:

Mater, ora Filium,
   That He will after this outlere
Nobis donet gaudium
   Sine fine for His mercy.   45
      Herefore I say:
   The mother of Mary, that merciful may,
Pray for us both night and day.

JAMES RYMAN

'Meekly We Sing and Say to Thee'

   Meekly we sing and say to thee,
   '*Maria, spes nostra, salue.*'

  Children of Eve, both great and small,
   Here in this vale of wretchedness
With great weeping to thee we call
   For help and grace in our distress,   5

And, as our tongues can express,
   Meekly we sing to thee,
   '*Maria, spes nostra, salue.*'

Thou art, lady, and ever shalt be,   10
   Queen of mercy, mother of grace;
Therefore at need, O lady free,
   Turn unto us thy glorious face
   And comfort us in every case,
      Since we do sing and say to thee,   15
      '*Maria, spes nostra, salue.*'

Though it be much that we offend,
   Yet we be thine for evermore;
Therefore thy grace to us extend,
   Pure virgin, after and before;   20
   For sin that we be not forlore,
      Since we do sing and say to thee,
      '*Maria, spes nostra, salue.*'

Thou dost abound so in all ways
   With goodness, grace, and all virtue,   25
So that our laud cannot suffice
   To thee, sweet mother of Jesu;
   But yet our prayers not eschew,
      Since we do sing and say to thee,
      '*Maria, spes nostra, salue.*'   30

Sweet and benign mediatrix,
   Thine eyen of grace on us thou cast,
Since thou art queen of paradise,
   And let not our hope be in waste,
   But show us thy Son at the last,   35
      Since we do sing and say to thee,
      '*Maria, spes nostra, salue.*'

O meek and mild, full of pity,
   For us pray to that Prince of Peace
That we may come to that city   40
   Whereof the joy shall never cease

But multiply and ever increase,
  Since we do sing and say to thee,
  'Maria, spes nostra, salue.'

ANON

'Noel, el, el, el, el, el, el . . .'

Noel, el, el, el, el, el, el, el, el, el, el, el,
Mary was greet with Gabriel.

Mary mother, meek and mild,
From shame and sin that ye us shield,
For great on ground ye gone with child,   5
  Gabriel nuntio.

Mary mother, be not adread:
Jesu is in your body bred,
And of your breast he will be fed
  Cum pudoris lilio.   10

Mary mother, the fruit of thee
For us was nailed on a tree;
In heaven is now His majesty:
  Fulget resurrectio.

Mary mother, the third day   15
Up He rose, as I you say;
To hell he took the right way,
  Motu fertur proprio.

Mary mother, after thine Son
Up thou styest with Him to wone;
The angels were glad when thou were come   20
  In coeli palatio.

ANON

'Mary Mother, Come and See'

'Mary mother, come and see:
Thy Son is nailed on a tree,
Hand and foot: He may not go,
His body is wounded all in woe.

'Thy sweet Son that thou hast born   5
To save mankind, that was forlorn,
His head is wreathen in a thorn;
His blissful body is all to-torn.'

When he this tale began to tell,
Mary would no longer dwell,   10
But hied her fast to that hill
Where Jesu His blood began to spill.

'Mine sweetè Son, that art me dear,
Why han men hanged Thee here?
Thy head is wreathen in a brier;   15
My lovely Son, where is Thine cheer?

'Thine sweetè body that in me rest,
Thine comely mouth that I have kissed!
Now on rood is made Thy nest:
Loved Child, what is me best?'   20

'Woman, to John I thee betake:
John, keep this woman for my sake.
For sinful souls my death I take;
On rood I hang for man his sake.

'This game alone me must play;   25
For sinful soul I die today;
There is none wight that goeth by the way
Of mine painès can well say.'

ANON

'What, Heard Ye Not?'

What, heard ye not? The King of Jerusalem
Is now born in Bethlehem.

I shall you tell a great marvel:
How an angel, for our avail,
Came to a maid and said, 'All hail!'   5

'All hail!' he said, and 'full of grace,
God is with thee now in this place;
A Child thou shalt bear in little space.'

'A Child?' she said, 'how may that be?
There had never no man knowledge of me.'   10
'The Holy Ghost,' he said, 'shall light in thee.'

'And, as thou art, so thou shalt be,'
The angel said, 'in virginity,
Before and after in every degree.'

The maid answered the angel again: 15
'If God will that this be sayen,
Thy words to me be full fain.'

Now will we all, in rejoicing
That we have heard this good tiding,
To that Child '*Te Deum*' sing.   20

ANON

'Flower of Roses, Angels' Joy'

Flower of roses, angels' joy,
Tower of David, ark of Noy;
   First of saints, whose true protecting
Of the young and weak in sprite
Makes my soul these lines indite   5
   To Thy throne her plaint directing.

Orphan child alone I lie,
Childlike to thee I cry,
   Queen of heaven, used to cherish;
Eyes of grace, behold, I fall;   10
Ears of pity, hear my call
   Lest in swaddling clouts I perish.

Hide the greatness of each fault;
My desert, if there be aught,
   By thy merits be enlarged   15
That the debts wherein I fall,
Paying nought but owing all,
   By thy prayer be discharged.

Pray to Him whose shape I bear,
By thy love, thy care, thy fear,   20
   By thy glorious birth and breeding,
That though our sins touch the sky
Yet His mercies mount more high,
   All His other works exceeding.

Tell Him that, in strengthening me   25
With His grace, He graceth thee,
   Every little one defending;
Tell Him that I cloy thine ears
With the cry of childish tears
   From His footstool still ascending.   30

Hear my cries and grant me aid,
Perfect mother, perfect maid;
    Hear my cries to thee addressed;
From my plaints turn not thy face,
Humble and yet full of grace,   35
    Pure, untouched, for ever blessed.

RICHARD EDWARDS

Amantium Irae Amoris Redintegratio

In going to my naked bed as one that would have slept,
I heard a wife sing to her child, that long before had
    wept.
She sighed sore and sang full sweet to bring the babe to
    rest,
That would not rest, but cried still, in sucking at her
    breast.
She was full weary of her watch and grieved with her
    child;   5
She rocked it and rated it until on her it smiled.
Then did she say, 'Now have I found the proverb true to
    prove,
The falling out of faithful friends is the renewing of love.'

Then took I paper, pen and ink, this proverb for to write,
In register for to remain of such a worthy wight.   10
As she proceeded thus in song unto her little brat,
Much matter uttered she of weight, in place whereas she
    sat;
And proved plain there was no beast, nor creature bearing
    life,
Could well be known to live in love without discord and
    strife.
Then kissed she her little babe and sware by God above, 15
'The falling out of faithful friends is the renewing of love.'

She said that neither king, ne prince, ne lord could live
    aright,
Until their puissance they did prove, their manhood and
    their might;
When manhood shall be matched so that fear can take no
    place,
Then weary works make warriors each other to embrace,   20
And leave their force that failed them, which did consume
    the rout,
That might before have lived their time and nature out.
Then did she sing as one that thought no man could her
    reprove,
'The falling out of faithful friends is the renewing of love.'

She said she saw no fish, ne fowl, ne beast within her
    haunt   25
That met a stranger in their kind, but could give it a
    taunt.
Since flesh might not endure, but rest must wrath succeed,
And force the fight to fall to play in pasture where they
    feed,
So noble nature can well end the works she hath begun,
And bridle well that will not cease, her tragedy in some.   30
Thus in her song she oft rehearsed, as did her well behove,
'The falling out of faithful friends is the renewing of love.'

'I marvel much, perdy!' (quoth she) 'for to behold the rout,
To see man, woman, boy and beast, to toss the world
    about.
Some kneel, some crouch, some beck, some check, and
    some can smoothly smile,   35
And some embrace others in arms, and there think many
    a wile.
Some stand aloof at cap and knee, some humble and some
    stout,
Yet are they never friends indeed until they once fall out.'
Thus ended she her song, and said, before she did remove,
'The falling out of faithful friends is the renewing of love.'   40

ARTHUR GOLDING, translator

[The Punishment of Niobe]

She falleth on the corpses cold and, taking no regard,
Bestowed her kisses on her sons as whom she afterward
Did know she never more should kiss. From whom she
    lifting tho
Her blue and bruised arms to heaven, said: 'O, thou cruel
    foe
Latona, feed, yea feed thyself, I say, upon my woe,   5
And overgorge thy stomach, yea, and glut thy cruel heart
With these my present painful pangs of bitter-griping
    smart.
In corpses seven I seven times dead am carried to my
    grave.
Rejoice, thou foe, and triumph now in that thou seemest
    to have
The upper hand. What? Upper hand? No, no, it is not so.   10
As wretched as my case doth seem, yet have I left me mo
Than thou for all thy happiness canst of thine own
    account.
Even after all these corpses, yet I still do thee surmount.'
Upon the end of these same words the twanging of the
    string
In letting of the arrow fly was clearly heard: which thing   15
Made everyone save Niobe afraid. Her heart was so
With sorrow hardened that she grew more bold. Her
    daughters tho
Were standing all mourning weed and hanging hair before
Their brothers' coffins. One of them, in pulling from the
    sore
An arrow sticking in his heart, sank down upon her
    brother   20
With mouth to mouth, and so did yield her fleeting ghost.
    Another
In comforting the wretched case and sorrow of her mother

Upon the sudden held her peace. She stricken was within
With double wound, which caused her her talking for to
  blin
And shut her mouth: but first her ghost was gone. One, all
  in vain   25
Attempting for to escape by flight was in her flying slain.
Another on her sister's corpse doth tumble down stark
  dead.
This quakes and trembles piteously, and she doth hide her
  head.
And when that six with sundry wounds dispatched were
  and gone,
At last as yet remained one; and, for to save that one,   30
Her mother with her body whole did cling about her fast,
And wrying her did over her her garments wholly cast,
And cried out: 'O leave me one: this little one yet save:
Of many but this only one the least of all I crave.'
But whiles she prayed, for whom she prayed was killed.
  Then down she sat   35
Bereft of all her children quite, and drawing to her fate,
Among her daughters and her sons and husband newly
  dead.
Her cheeks waxed hard; the air could stir no hair upon her
  head;
The colour of her face was dim and clearly void of blood,
And sadly under open lids her eyes unmoved stood.   40
In all her body was no life, for even her very tongue
And palate of her mouth was hard, and each to other
  clung.
Her pulses ceased for to beat; her neck did cease to bow;
Her arms to stir, her feet to go, all power forewent as now;
And into stone her very womb and bowels also bind.   45
But yet she wept, and, being hoist by force of whirling
  wind,
Was carried into Phrygia. There upon a mountain's top
She weepeth still in stone. From stone the dreary tears do
  drop . . .

EDMUND SPENSER

[Charissa]

. . . By this, Charissa, late in child-bed brought,
　Was waxen strong, and left her fruitful nest;
To her fair Una brought this unacquainted guest.

She was a woman in her freshest age,
　Of freshest beauty, and of bounty rare,   5
　With goodly grace and comely personage,
　That was on earth not easy to compare:
　Full of great love, but Cupid's wanton snare
　As hell she hated, chaste in work and will.
　Her neck and breasts were ever open bare,   10
　That aye thereof her babes might suck their fill;
The rest was all in yellow robes arrayed still.

A multitude of babes about her hung,
　Playing their sports, that joyed her to behold,
　Whom still she fed whiles they were weak and young,   15
　But thrust them forth still as they waxed old:
　And on her head she wore a tiara of gold,
　Adorned with gems and ouches wondrous fair,
　Whose passing price uneath was to be told;
　And by her side there sat a gentle pair   20
Of turtle doves, she sitting in an ivory chair.

The knight and Una, entering, fair her greet,
　And bid her joy of that her happy brood;
　Who them requites with courtesies seeming meet,
　And entertains with friendly cheerful mood . . .   25

NICHOLAS BRETON

A Sweet Lullaby

Come, little babe, come, silly soul,
Thy father's shame, thy mother's grief,
Born, as I doubt, to all our dole,
And to thyself unhappy chief;
    Sing lullaby and lap it warm,   5
    Poor soul that thinks no creature harm.

Thou little think'st and less dost know
The cause of this thy mother's moan;
Thou want'st the wit to wail her woe,
And I myself am all alone;   10
    Why dost thou weep? why dost thou wail,
    And knowest not yet what thou dost ail?

Come, little wretch! Ah, silly heart!
Mine only joy, what can I more?
If there be any wrong thy smart,   15
That may the destinies implore,
    'Twas I, I say, against my will:
    I wail the time, but be thou still.

And dost thou smile? Oh, thy sweet face!
Would God Himself He might thee see!   20
No doubt thou wouldst soon purchase grace,
I know right well, for thee and me:
    But come to mother, babe, and play,
    For father false is fled away.

Sweet boy, if it by fortune chance   25
Thy father home again to send,
If death do strike me with his lance,
Yet may'st thou me to him commend.
    If any ask thy mother's name,
    Tell how by love she purchased blame.   30

Then will his gentle heart soon yield;
I know him of a noble mind;
Although a lion in the field,
A lamb in town thou shalt him find:
   Ask blessing, babe, be not afraid!   35
   His sugared words hath me betrayed.

Then may'st thou joy and be right glad,
Although in woe I seem to moan;
Thy father is no rascal lad,
A noble youth of blood and bone: 40
   His glancing looks, if he once smile,
   Right honest women may beguile.

Come, little boy, and rock asleep!
Sing lullaby, and be thou still!
I, that can do nought else but weep,
Will sit by thee and wail my fill: 45
   God bless my babe, and lullaby,
   From this thy father's quality.

JOHN HARINGTON

To His Mother

There was a battle fought of late,
   Yet was the slaughter small;
The strife was whether I should write,
   Or send nothing at all.
Of one side were the captains' names   5
   Short Time and Little Skill;
One fought alone against them both,
   Whose name was Great Good-will.
Short Time enforced me in a strait,
   And bade me hold my hand;
Small Skill also withstood desire   10
   My writing to withstand.

But Great Good-will, in show though small,
  To write encouraged me,
And to the battle held on still,   15
  No common thing to see.
Thus 'gan these busy warriors three
  Between themselves to fight
As valiantly as though they had
  Been of much greater might.   20
Till Fortune, that unconstant dame,
  Which rules such things alway,
Did cause the weaker part in fight
  To bear the greater sway.
And then the victor caused me,   25
  However was my skill,
To write these verses unto you
  To show my great good-will.

ROBERT GREENE

'Weep Not, My Wanton'

Weep not, my wanton, smile upon my knee;
When thou art old, there's grief enough for thee,
  Mother's wag, pretty boy,
  Father's sorrow, father's joy.
  When thy father first did see   5
  Such a boy by him and me,
  He was glad, I was woe:
  Fortune changed made him so,
  When he left his pretty boy,
  Last his sorrow, first his joy.   10

Weep not, my wanton, smile upon my knee;
When thou art old there's grief enough for thee.
  Streaming tears that never stint,
  Like pearl drops from a flint,
  Fell by course from his eyes,   15

That one another's place supplies:
Thus he grieved in every part,
Tears of blood fell from his heart,
When he left his pretty boy,
Father's sorrow, father's joy.   20

Weep not my wanton, smile upon my knee;
When thou art old, there's grief enough for thee.
The wanton smiled, father wept;
Mother cried, baby leapt;
More he crowed, more we cried;   25
Nature could not sorrow hide.
He must go, he must kiss
Child and mother, baby bliss;
For he left his pretty boy,
Father's sorrow, father's joy.   30

Weep not, my wanton, smile upon my knee;
When thou art old there's grief enough for thee.

EMILIA LANIER

[A Defence of Eve]

Now Pontius Pilate is to judge the cause
Of faultless Jesus, who before him stands,
Who neither hath offended prince nor laws,
Although He now be brought in woeful bands.
O noble governor, make thou yet a pause: 5
Do not in innocent blood imbrue thy hands,
    But hear the words of thy most worthy wife,
    Who sends to thee to beg her Saviour's life.

Let barbarous cruelty far depart from thee,
And in true justice take affliction's part;
Open thine eyes, that thou the truth may'st see: 10
Do not the thing that goes against thy heart;

Condemn not Him that must thy Saviour be,
But view His holy life, His good desert.
   Let not us women glory in men's fall,   15
   Who had power given to overrule us all.

Till now your indiscretion sets us free
And makes our former faults much less appear:
Our mother Eve, who tasted of the tree,
Giving to Adam what she held most dear,   20
Was simply good, and had no power to see:
The aftercoming harm did not appear.
   The subtle serpent that our sex betrayed
   Before the Fall so sure a plot had laid

That undiscerning ignorance perceived   25
No guile nor craft that was by him intended;
For had she known of what we were bereaved,
To his request she had not condescended.
But she, poor soul, by cunning was deceived:
No hurt therein her harmless heart intended;   30
   For she alleged God's word, which he denies,
   That they should die, but even as gods be wise.

But surely Adam cannot be excused:
Her fault though great, yet he was most to blame:
What weakness offered, strength might have refused.   35
Being lord of all, the greater was his shame:
Although the serpent's craft had her abused,
God's holy word ought all his actions frame;
   For he was lord and king of all the earth
   Before poor Eve had either life or breath.   40

Who, being framed by God's eternal hand,
The perfect'st man that ever breathed on earth;
And from God's mouth received the strait command,
The breath whereof he knew was present death:
Yea, having power to rule both sea and land,   45
Yet with one apple won to lose that breath
   Which God had breathed on his beauteous face,
   Bringing us all in danger and disgrace.

And then to lay the fault on patience's back,
That we, poor women, must endure it all! 50
We know right well he did discretion lack,
Being not persuaded thereunto at all.
If Eve did err, it was for knowledge's sake;
The fruit, being fair, persuaded him to fall:
 No subtle serpent's falsehood did betray him; 55
 If he would eat it, who had power to stay him?

Not Eve, whose fault was only too much love,
Which made her give this present to her dear,
That what she tasted he likewise might prove,
Whereby his knowledge might become more clear: 60
He never sought her weakness to reprove
With those sharp words which he of God did hear.
 Yet men will boast of knowledge, which he took
 From Eve's fair hand, as from a learned book.

If any evil did in her remain,
Being made of him, he was the ground of all: 65
If one of many worlds could lay a stain
Upon our sex, and work so great a fall
To wretched man by Satan's subtle train,
What will so foul a fault amongst you all? 70
 Her weakness did the serpent's words obey,
 But you in malice God's dear Son betray . . .

BEN JONSON

Epigram 22: On My First Daughter

Here lies to each her parents' ruth,
Mary, the daughter of their youth:
Yet, all heaven's gifts, being heaven's due,
It makes the father less to rue.
At six months' end she parted hence 5
With safety of her innocence;

Whose soul heaven's queen (whose name she bears),
In comfort of her mother's tears,
Hath placed amongst her virgin train:
Where, while that severed doth remain,   10
This grave partakes the fleshly birth.
Which cover lightly, gentle earth.

Epigram 62: To Fine Lady Would-be

Fine Madam Would-be, wherefore should you fear,
That love to make so well, a child to bear?
The world reputes you barren; but I know
Your 'pothecary, and his drug, says no.
Is it the pain affrights? That's soon forgot.   5
Or your complexion's loss? You have a pot
That can restore that. Will it hurt your feature?
To make amends, you're thought a wholesome creature.
What should the cause be? Oh, you live at court:
And there's both loss of time, and loss of sport   10
In a great belly. Write, then, on thy womb:
Of the not born, yet buried, here's the tomb.

WILLIAM BROWNE OF TAVISTOCK

[Epitaph]

Underneath this sable hearse
Lies the subject of all verse:
Sidney's sister, Pembroke's mother:
Death, ere thou hast slain another,
Fair and learned and good as she,   5
Time shall throw a dart at thee.

Marble piles let no man raise
To her name for after days;
Some kind woman born as she,
Reading this, like Niobe,
Shall turn marble, and become   10
Both her mourner and her tomb.

ROBERT HERRICK

To Dianeme. A Ceremony in Gloucester

I'll to thee a simnel bring
'Gainst thou goest a-Mothering,
So that, when she blesseth thee,
Half that blessing thou'lt give me.

FRANCIS QUARLES

On the Infancy of Our Saviour

Hail, blessed Virgin, full of heavenly grace,
Blest above all that sprang from human race;
Whose heaven-saluted womb brought forth in one
A blessed Saviour and a blessed Son.
Oh, what a ravishment it had been to see   5
Thy little Saviour perking on thy knee!
To see Him nuzzle in thy virgin-breast,
His milk-white body all unclad, undressed!
To see thy busy fingers clothe and wrap
His spreading limbs in thy indulgent lap!
To see His desperate eyes with childish grace   10
Smiling upon His smiling mother's face!
And when his forward strength began to bloom,
To see Him diddle up and down the room!

Oh, who would think so sweet a Babe as this 15
Should e'er be slain by a false-hearted kiss!
Had I a rag, if, sure, Thy body wore it,
Pardon, sweet Babe, I think I should adore it!
Till then, O grant this boon (a boon, or dearer),
The weed not being, I may adore the wearer. 20

RACHEL SPEIGHT

from **The Dream**

Thus leaving them I passed on my way;
But ere that I had little further gone,
I saw a fierce insatiable foe,
Depopulating countries, sparing none:
Without respect of age, sex, or degree, 5
It did devour, and could not daunted be.

Some feared this foe, some loved it as a friend;
For though none could the force of it withstand,
Yet some by it were sent to Tophet's flames,
But others led to heavenly Canaan land: 10
On some it seized with a gentle power,
And others furiously it did devour.

The name of this impartial foe was Death,
Whose rigour, whilst I furiously did view,
Upon a sudden, ere I was aware, 15
With piercing dart my mother dear it slew,
Which, when I saw, it made me so to weep
That tears and sobs did rouse me from my sleep.

But, when I waked, I found my dream was true;
For Death had ta'en my mother's breath away, 20
Though of her life it could not her bereave,
Since she in glory lives with Christ for aye;

Which makes me glad, and thankful for her bliss,
Though still bewail her absence whom I miss.

A sudden sorrow pierceth to the quick;   25
Speedy encounters fortitude doth try;
Unarmed men receive the deepest wound,
Expected perils time doth lenify;
Her sudden loss hath cut my feeble heart
So deep that daily I endure the smart.   30

THOMAS RANDOLPH

In Praise of Women in General

He is a parricide to his mother's name,
And with an impious hand murders her fame,
That wrongs the praise of women: that dares write
Libels on saints, or with foul ink requite
The milk they lent us. Better sex, command   5
To your defence my more religious hand
At sword, or pen: yours was the nobler birth,
For you of man were made, man but of earth,
The son of dust; and though your sin did breed
His fall, again you raised him in your seed: 10
Adam in his sleep a gainful loss sustained,
That for one rib a better self regained;
Who, had he not your blest creation seen,
An anchorite in paradise had been.
Why in this work did the creation rest,   15
But that eternal providence thought you best
Of all his six days' labour? Beasts should do
Homage to man, but man should wait on you.
You are of comelier sight, of daintier touch,
A tender flesh, a colour bright, and such   20
As Parians see in marble; skin more fair,
More glorious head, and far more glorious hair,
Eyes full of grace and quickness; purer roses

Blush in your cheeks; a milder white composes
Your stately fronts; your breath more sweet than his   25
Breathes spice, and nectar drops at every kiss.
Your skins are smooth, bristles on theirs do grow
Like quills of porcupines; rough wool doth flow
O'er all their faces, you approach more near
The form of angels; they like beasts appear.   30
If then in bodies where the souls do dwell
You better us, do then our souls excel?
No; we in soul's equal perfection see
There can in them nor male nor female be.
Boast we of knowledge? You have more than we: 35
You were the first ventured to pluck the tree.
And, that more rhetoric in your tongues doth lie,
Let him dispute against that dares deny
Your least commands, and not persuaded be
With Samson's strength and David's piety   40
To be your willing captives. Virtue sure
Were blind as Fortune, should she choose the poor
Rough cottage man to live in, and despise
To dwell in you, the stately edifice.
Thus you are proved the better sex, and we   45
Must all repent that in our pedigree
We choose the father's name, where, should we take
The mother's (a more honoured blood), 'twould make
Our generation sure and certain be,
And I'd believe some faith in heraldry!   50
Thus, perfect creatures, if detraction rise
Against your sex, dispute but with your eyes,
Your hand, your lip, your brow: there will be sent
So subtle and so strong an argument,
Will teach the Stoic his affection too,   55
And call the Cynic from his tub to woo.
Thus mustering up your beauteous troops, go on:
The fairest is the valiant Amazon.

ANNE BRADSTREET

from **The Four Ages of Man (Childhood)**

Ah me! conceived in sin, and born in sorrow:
A nothing; here today but gone tomorrow.
Whose mean beginning blushing can't reveal,
But night and darkness must with shame conceal.
My mother's breeding sickness I will spare;   5
Her nine months' weary burden not declare.
To show her bearing pangs I should do wrong,
To tell that pain which can't be told by tongue.
With tears into this world I did arrive;
My mother still did waste, as I did thrive: 10
Who yet with love, and all alacrity,
Spending was willing to be spent for me:
With wayward cries I did disturb her rest,
Who sought still to appease me with her breast:
With weary arms she danced, and 'bye, bye' sung   15
When wretched I (ungrate) had done the
    wrong . . .

Before the Birth of One of Her Children

All things within this fading world hath end,
Adversity doth still our joys attend;
No ties so strong, no friends so clear and sweet,
But with death's parting blow is sure to meet.
The sentence past is most irrevocable,   5
A common thing yet, oh, inevitable;
How soon, my dear, death may my steps attend,
How soon it may be thy lot to lose thy friend,
We both are ignorant; yet love bids me
These farewell lines to recommend to thee,   10

That when that knot's untied that made us one,
I may seem thine, who in effect am none.
And if I see not half my days that's due,
What nature would, God grant to yours and you;
The many faults that well you know I have,   15
Let be interred in my oblivious grave;
If any worth or virtue were in me,
Let that live freshly in thy memory
And when thou feelest no grief, as I no harms,
Yet love thy dead, who long lay in thine arms: 20
And when thy loss shall be repaid with gains,
Look to my little babes, my dear remains.
And if thou love thyself, or loved'st me,
These O protect from stepdame's injury.
And if Chance to thine eyes shall bring this verse,   25
With some sad sighs honour my absent hearse;
And kiss this paper for thy love's dear sake,
Who with salt tears this last farewell did take.

HENRY VAUGHAN

from **The Tempest**

When Nature on her bosom saw
    Her infants die,
And all her flowers withered to straw,
    Her breasts grown dry,
She made the earth, their nurse and tomb,   5
    Sigh to the sky,
'Til to those sighs fetched from her womb
    Rain did reply:
So, in the midst of all her fears
    And faint requests,   10
Her earnest sighs procured her tears
    And filled her breasts.

KATHERINE PHILIPS

Epitaph: On Her Son H.P., at St Syth's Church, Where Her Body Also Lies Interred

What on earth deserves our trust?
Youth and beauty both are dust.
Long we gathering are with pain,
What one moment calls again.
Seven years' childless marriage past,   5
A son, a son is born at last:
So exactly limned and fair,
Full of good spirits, mien, and air
As a long life promised;
Yet, in no less than six weeks, dead.   10
Too promising, too great a mind,
In so small room to be confined;
Therefore, as fit in heaven to dwell,
He quickly broke the prison shell.
So the subtle alchemist   15
Can't with Hermes'-seal resist
The powerful spirit's subtler flight,
But 'twill bid him long good night.
And so the sun, if it arise
Half so glorious as his eyes,   20
Like this infant, takes a shroud,
Buried in a morning cloud.

THOMAS CREECH, translator

[Mother Venus]

Kind Venus, glory of the blest abodes,
Parent of Rome, and joy of men and gods;
Delight of all, comfort of sea and earth;
To whose kind powers all creatures owe their birth.
At thy approach, great goddess, straight remove   5
Whate'er are rough, and enemies to love:
The clouds disperse, the winds do swiftly waste,
And reverently in murmurs breathe their last;
The earth with various art (for thy warm powers
That dull mass feels) puts forth their gaudy flowers: 10
For thee doth subtle Luxury prepare
The choicest stores of earth, of sea, and air;
To welcome thee she comes profusely dressed
With all the spices of the wanton east;
To pleasure thee e'en lazy Luxury toils.   15
The roughest sea puts on smooth looks, and smiles;
The well-pleased heaven assumes a brighter ray
At thy approach, and makes a double day.
    When first the gentle spring begins to inspire
Melting thoughts, soft wishes, gay desire,   20
And warm Favonius fans the amorous fire,
First through the birds the active flame doth move,
Who, with their mates, sit down, and sing, and love;
They gratefully their tuneful voice employ
At thy approach, the author of their joy.   25
Each beast forgets his rage, and entertains
A softer fury: through the flowery plains,
Through rapid streams, through woods and silent groves
With wanton play they run to meet their loves.
Whole Nature yields unto your charms: the ways   30
You lead, she follows, and eagerly obeys.
Acted by those kind principles you infuse,
Each bird and beast endeavours to produce
His kind, and the decaying world renews . . .

AMBROSE PHILIPS

To Miss Charlotte Pulteney in Her Mother's Arms, 1 May 1724

Timely blossom, infant fair,
Fondling of a happy pair,
Every morn, and every night,
Their solicitous delight,
Sleeping, waking, still at ease,   5
Pleasing, without skill to please,
Little gossip, blithe and hale,
Tattling many a broken tale,
Singing many a tuneless song,
Lavish of a heedless tongue,   10
Simple maiden, void of art,
Babbling out the very heart,
Yet abandoned to thy will,
Yet imagining no ill,
Yet too innocent to blush,   15
Like the linlet in the bush,
To the mother-linnet's note
Moduling her slender throat,
Chirping forth thy petty joys,
Wanton in the change of toys,   20
Like the linnet green, in May,
Flitting to each bloomy spray,
Wearied then, and glad of rest,
Like the linlet in the nest.
This thy present happy lot,   25
This, in time, will be forgot:
Other pleasures, other cares,
Ever-busy time prepares;
And thou shalt in thy daughter see,
This picture, once, resembled thee.   30

MARY BARBER

Written for My Son, and Spoken by Him at His First Putting on Breeches

What is it our mammas bewitches,
To plague us little boys with breeches?
To tyrant custom we must yield
Whilst vanquished Reason flies the field.
Our legs must suffer by ligation,   5
To keep the blood from circulation;
And then our feet, though young and tender,
We to the shoemaker surrender,
Who often makes our shoes so strait
Our growing feet they cramp and fret;   10
Whilst, with contrivance most profound,
Across our insteps we are bound,
Which is the cause, I make no doubt,
Why thousands suffer in the gout.
Our wiser ancestors wore brogues,   15
Before the surgeons bribed these rogues
With narrow toes and heels like pegs
To help to make us break our legs.

Then, ere we know how to use our fists,
Our mothers closely bind our wrists,   20
And never think our clothes are neat
Till they're so tight we cannot eat.
And, to increase our other pains,
The hat-band helps to cramp our brains.
The cravat finishes the work,   25
Like bowstring sent from the Grand Turk.

Thus dress, that should prolong our date,
Is made to hasten on our fate.
Fair privilege of nobler natures,
To be more plagued than other creatures!   30

The wild inhabitants of air
Are clothed by heaven with wondrous care:
The beauteous, well-compacted feathers
Are coats of mail against all weathers;
Enamelled, to delight the eye,   35
Gay as the bow that decks the sky.
The beasts are clothed with beauteous skins;
The fishes armed with scales and fins,
Whose lustre lends the sailor light
When all the stars are hid in night.   40

    Oh, were our dress contrived like these,
For use, for ornament, and ease!
Man only seems to sorrow born,
Naked, defenceless, and forlorn.

    Yet we have Reason to supply   45
What nature did to man deny:
Weak viceroy! Who thy power will own
When Custom has usurped thy throne?
In vain did I appeal to thee
Ere I would wear his livery;   50
Who, in defiance of thy rules,
Delights to make us act like fools.
O'er human race the tyrant reigns,
And binds them in eternal chains.
We yield to his despotic sway,   55
The only monarch all obey.

MEHETABEL WRIGHT

To an Infant Expiring the Second Day of its Birth

Tender softness, infant mild,
Perfect, purest, brightest child;
Transient lustre, beauteous clay,

Smiling wonder of a day:
Ere the last convulsive start   5
Rends thy unresisting heart;
Ere the long-enduring swoon
Weighs thy precious eyelids down;
Oh, regard a mother's moan,
Anguish deeper than thy own!   10
Fairest eyes, whose dawning light
Late with rapture blessed my sight,
Ere your orbs extinguished be,
Bend their trembling beams on me;
Drooping sweetness, verdant flower,   15
Blooming, withering in an hour,
Ere thy gentle breast sustains
Latest, fiercest, vital pains,
Hear a suppliant! Let me be
Partner in thy destiny!   20

ELIZABETH BOYD

On the Death of an Infant of Five Days Old, Being a Beautiful but Abortive Birth

How frail is human life! How fleet our breath,
Born with the symptoms of approaching death!
What dire convulsions rend a mother's breast
When by a first-born son's decease distressed.
Although an embryo, an abortive boy,   5
Thy wondrous beauties give a wondrous joy:
Still flattering hope a flattering idea gives,
And, whilst the birth can breathe, we say it lives.
With what kind warmth the dear-loved babe was pressed:
The darling man was with less love caressed!   10
How dear, how innocent, the fond embrace!
The father's form all o'er, the father's face,
The sparkling eye, gay with a cherub smile,

Some flying hours the mother-pangs beguile;
The pretty mouth a Cupid's tale expressed,   15
In amorous murmurs, to the full-swollen breast.
If angel infancy can so endear,
Dear angel-infants must command a tear.
Oh! could the stern-souled sex but know the pain,
Or the soft mother's agonies sustain,   20
With tenderest love the obdurate heart would burn,
And the shocked father tear for tear return.

WILLIAM COWPER

On the Receipt of My Mother's Picture Out of Norfolk, The Gift of My Cousin Ann Bodham

Oh that those lips had language! Life has passed
With me but roughly since I heard thee last.
Those lips are thine – thy own sweet smiles I see,
The same that oft in childhood solaced me;
Voice only fails, else, how distinct they say,   5
'Grieve not, my child, chase all thy fears away!'
The meek intelligence of those dear eyes
(Blest be the art that can immortalise,
The art that baffles Time's tyrannic claim
To quench it) here shines on me still the same.   10
   Faithful remembrancer of one so dear,
O welcome guest, though unexpected, here!
Who bidd'st me honour with an artless song,
Affectionate, a mother lost so long:
I will obey, not willingly alone,   15
But gladly, as the precept were her own;
And, while that face renews my filial grief,
Fancy shall weave a charm for my relief –
Shall steep me in Elysian reverie,
A momentary dream, that thou art she.   20

My mother! when I learned that thou wast dead,
Say, wast thou conscious of the tears I shed?
Hovered thy spirit o'er thy sorrowing son,
Wretch even then, life's journey just begun?
Perhaps thou gavest me, though unseen, a kiss;   25
Perhaps a tear, if souls can weep in bliss –
Ah that maternal smile! It answers – Yes.
I heard the bell tolled on thy burial day.
I saw the hearse that bore thee slow away,
And, turning from my nursery window, drew   30
A long, long sigh, and wept a last adieu!
But was it such? – It was. – Where thou art gone
Adieus and farewells are a sound unknown.
May I but meet thee on that peaceful shore,
The parting sound shall pass my lips no more!   35
Thy maidens grieved themselves at my concern,
Oft gave me promise of a quick return.
What ardently I wished, I long believed,
And, disappointed still, was still deceived;
By disappointment every day beguiled,   40
Dupe of tomorrow, even from a child.
Thus many a sad tomorrow came and went,
Till, all my stock of infant sorrow spent,
I learned at last submission to my lot;
But, though I less deplored thee, ne'er forgot.   45
   Where once we dwelt our name is heard no more,
Children not thine have trod my nursery floor;
And where the gardener, Robin, day by day,
Drew me to school along the public way,
Delighted with my bauble coach, and wrapped   50
In scarlet mantle warm, and velvet capped,
'Tis now become a history little known
That once we called the pastoral house our own:
Short-lived possession! But the record fair
That memory keeps of all thy kindness there,   55
Still outlives many a storm that has effaced
A thousand other themes less deeply traced.
Thy nightly visits to my chamber made,
That thou mightest know me safe and warmly laid;
Thy morning bounties ere I left my home,   60

The biscuit or confectionary plum;
The fragrant waters on my cheeks bestowed
By thy own hand, till fresh they shone and glowed;
All this, and more endearing still than all,
Thy constant flow of love that knew no fall,   65
Ne'er roughened by those cataracts and brakes
That humour interposed too often makes;
All this still legible in memory's page,
And still to be so, to my latest age,
Adds joy to duty, makes me glad to pay   70
Such honours to thee as my numbers may;
Perhaps a frail memorial, but sincere,
Not scorned in heaven, though little noticed here.
    Could Time, his flight reversed, restore the hours
When, playing with thy vesture's tissued flowers,   75
The violet, the pink, and jessamine,
I pricked them into paper with a pin
(And thou wast happier than myself the while,
Would'st softly speak, and stroke my head, and smile):
Could those few pleasant hours again appear,   80
Might one wish bring them, would I wish them here?
I would not trust my heart – the dear delight
Seems so to be desired, perhaps I might.
But no – what here we call our life is such,
So little to be loved, and thou so much,   85
That I should ill requite thee to constrain
Thy unbound spirit into bonds again.
    Thou, as a gallant bark from Albion's coast
(The storms all weathered, and the ocean crossed)
Shoots into port at some well-havened isle,   90
Where spices breathe and brighter seasons smile,
There sits quiescent on the floods that show
Her beauteous form reflected clear below,
While airs impregnated with incense play
Around her, fanning light her streamers gay;   95
So thou, with sails how swift, hast reached the shore
'Where tempests never beat, nor billows roar,'
And thy loved consort on the dangerous tide
Of life, long since, has anchored at thy side.

But me, scarce hoping to attain that rest,   100
Always from port withheld, always distressed –
Me howling winds drive devious, tempest tossed,
Sails ripped, seams opening wide, and compass lost,
And day by day some current's thwarting force
Sets me more distant from a prosperous course.   105
But oh the thought, that thou art safe, and he!
That thought is joy, arrive what may to me.
My boast is not that I deduce my birth
From loins enthroned, and rulers of the earth;
But higher far my proud pretensions rise –   110
The son of parents passed into the skies.
And now, farewell – Time, unrevoked, has run
His wonted course, yet what I wished is done.
By contemplation's help, not sought in vain,
I seem to have lived my childhood o'er again;   115
To have renewed the joys that once were mine,
Without the sin of violating thine:
And, while the wings of fancy still are free,
And I can view this mimic show of thee,
Time has but half succeeded in his theft –   120
Thyself removed, thy power to soothe me left.

ANNE HUNTER

A Pastoral Song

My mother bids me bind my hair
    With bands of rosy hue,
Tie up my sleeves with ribbons rare,
    And lace my bodice blue.

'For why,' she cries, 'sit still and weep   5
    While others dance and play?'
Alas! I scarce can go or creep
    While Lubin is away.

'Tis sad to think the days are gone
   When those we love were near;   10
I sit upon this mossy stone,
   And sigh when none can hear.

And while I spin my flaxen thread,
   And sing my simple lay,
The village seems asleep, or dead,   15
   Now Lubin is away.

ANNA LAETITIA BARBAULD

from **Washing Day**

                 Woe to the friend
Whose evil stars have urged him forth to claim
On such a day the hospitable rites!
Looks, blank at best, and stinted courtesy,
Shall he receive. Vainly he feeds his hopes   5
With dinner of roast chicken, savoury pie,
Or tart or pudding: pudding he nor tart
That day shall eat; nor, though the husband try,
Mending what can't be helped, to kindle mirth
From cheer deficient, shall his consort's brow   10
Clear up propitious: the unlucky guest
In silence dines, and early slinks away.
I well remember, when a child, the awe
This day struck into me; for then the maids,
I scarce knew why, looked cross, and drove me from them;   15
Nor soft caress could I obtain, nor hope
Usual indulgences: jelly or creams,
Relic of costly suppers, and set by
For me, their petted one; or buttered toast,
When butter was forbid; or thrilling tale   20
Of ghost, or witch, or murder. So I went
And sheltered me beside the parlour fire:
There my dear grandmother, eldest of forms,

Tended the little ones, and watched from harm,
Anxiously fond, though oft her spectacles   25
With elfin cunning hid, and oft the pins
Drawn from her ravelled stocking, might have soured
One less indulgent. –
At intervals my mother's voice was heard,
Urging dispatch. Briskly the work went on,   30
All hands employed to wash, to rinse, to wring,
To fold, and starch, and clap, and iron, and plait.
Then would I sit me down, and ponder much
Why washings were. Sometimes through hollow bowl
Of pipe amused we blew, and sent aloft   35
The floating bubbles, little dreaming then
To see, Montgolfier, thy silken ball
Ride buoyant through the clouds – so near approach
The sports of children and the toils of men.
Earth, air, and sky, and ocean, hath its bubbles,   40
And verse is one of them – this most of all.

To a Little Invisible Being Who is Expected Soon to Become Visible

Germ of new life, whose powers expanding slow
For many a moon their full perfection wait –
Haste, precious pledge of happy love, to go
Auspicious borne through life's mysterious gate.

What powers lie folded in thy curious frame –   5
Senses from objects locked, and mind from thought!
How little canst thou guess thy lofty claim
To grasp at all the worlds the Almighty wrought!

And see, the genial season's warmth to share,
Fresh younglings shoot, and opening roses glow!   10
Swarms of new life exulting fill the air –
Haste, infant bud of being, haste to blow!

For thee the nurse prepares her lulling songs,
The eager matrons count the lingering day;
But far the most thy anxious parent longs   15
On thy soft cheek a mother's kiss to lay.

She only asks to lay her burden down,
That her glad arms that burden may resume;
And nature's sharpest pangs her wishes crown,
That free thee living from thy living tomb.   20

She longs to fold to her maternal breast
Part of herself, yet to herself unknown;
To see and to salute the stranger guest,
Fed with her life through many a tedious moon.

Come, reap thy rich inheritance of love!   25
Bask in the fondness of a mother's eye!
Nor wit nor eloquence her heart shall move
Like the first accents of thy feeble cry.

Haste, little captive, burst thy prison doors!
Launch on the living world, and spring to light!   30
Nature for thee displays her various stores,
Opens her thousand inlets of delight.

If charmed verse or muttered prayers had power
With favouring spells to speed thee on thy way,
Anxious I'd bid my beads each passing hour,   35
Till thy wished smile thy mother's pangs o'erpay.

ANN YEARSLEY

To Mira, On the Care of Her Infant

Mira, as thy dear Edward's senses grow,
Be sure they all will seek this point – *to know.*

Woo to enquiry – strictures long avoid;
By force the thirst of weakly sense is cloyed:
Silent attend the frown, the gaze, the smile,   5
To grasp far objects the incessant toil;
So play life's springs with energy, and try
The unceasing thirst of knowledge to supply.
    I saw the beauteous Caleb t' other day
Stretch forth his little hand to touch a spray,   10
Whilst on the grass his drowsy nurse inhaled
The sweets of nature as her sweets exhaled.
But, ere the infant reached the playful leaf,
She pulled him back – his eyes o'erflowed with grief;
He checked his tears – her fiercer passions strove,   15
She looked a vulture cowering o'er a dove!
'I'll teach you, brat!' The pretty trembler sighed –
When, with a cruel shake, she hoarsely cried –
'Your mother spoils you – everything you see
You covet. It shall ne'er be so with me!   20
Here, eat this cake, sit still, and don't you rise –
Why don't you pluck the sun down from the skies?
I'll spoil your sport – Come, laugh me in the face –
And henceforth learn to keep your proper place.
You rule me in the house! To hush your noise   25
I, like a spaniel, must run for toys:
But here, sir, let the trees alone, nor cry –
Pluck if you dare – Who's master, you or I?'
    Oh brutal force, to check the enquiring mind
When it would pleasure in a rosebud find!   30

JANE CAVE

An Elegy on a Maiden Name

Adieu, dear name, which birth and nature gave –
Lo, at the altar I've interred dear CAVE;
For there it fell, expired, and found a grave.

Forgive, dear spouse, this ill-timed tear or two,
They are not meant in disrespect to you;   5
I hope the name which you have lately given
Was kindly meant, and sent to me by heaven.
But ah! the loss of CAVE I must deplore,
For that dear name the tenderest mother bore.
With that she passed full forty years of life,   10
Adorned the important character of wife:
Then meet for bliss from earth to heaven retired,
With holy zeal and true devotion fired.

In me what blessed my father may you find,
A wife domestic, virtuous, meek, and kind.   15
What blessed my mother may I meet in you,
A friend and husband – faithful, wise, and true.

Then be our voyage prosperous or adverse,
No keen upbraiding shall our tongues rehearse;
But mutually we'll brave against the storm,   20
Remembering still for helpmates we were born.
Then let rough torrents roar or skies look dark,
If love commands the helm which guides our bark,
No shipwreck will we fear, but to the end
Each find in each a just, unshaken friend.   25

Written a Few Hours Before the Birth of a Child

My God, prepare me for that hour
    When most thy aid I want;
Uphold me by thy mighty power,
    Nor let my spirits faint.

I ask not life, I ask not ease,   5
    But patience to submit
To what shall best thy goodness please,
    Then come what thou seest fit.

Come pain, or agony, or death,
  If such the will divine;   10
With joy shall I give up my breath,
  If resignation's mine.

One wish to name I'd humbly dare,
  If death thy pleasure be:
O may the harmless babe I bear   15
  Haply expire with me.

HANNAH WALLIS

The Female's Lamentations; or, The Village in Mourning

Once more I visited the place
  Where first I drew my breath;
But oh! what desolation made
  By that grim monster Death!

There hardly was a building here,   5
  But some kind friend was gone;
And former joys are turned to pain
  When this is thought upon.

I went and viewed that empty house
  Where my late brother dwelt;   10
A wife and offspring he has left:
  Oh the keen grief I felt!

And walking on I cast a look
  Upon that empty Hall;
Those friends that once lived there are dead: 15
  'Tis all in vain to call.

And did I see the mansion where
　　His Honour once did dwell?
Ye poor, that did receive his gifts,
　　'Tis vain your wants to tell.   20

For now he slumbers in the dust,
　　Regardless of your cry:
Each empty room bespeaks your loss,
　　Those gardens ruined lie.

Oh, where is now the pleasure which   25
　　Once sparkled in each face?
The widow's heart sure sung for joy:
　　How cheerful was that place!

The mother here her garments showed,
　　The father told the son;   30
His Honour did their schooling pay;
　　What good his spouse has done!

But now the village seems to mourn,
　　And that remark is just:
'Oh, put no confidence in man,   35
　　Do not in princes trust.'

I only had to cross the Green
　　Where once my parents lived;
The owner of that dwelling now
　　Did me refreshment give.   40

I in the garden saw the trees
　　My own dear brother bought;
And though they live, yet he is dead:
　　How mournful was the thought!

Here is the orchard, where I, with   45
　　My sister, oft did walk;
With pleasure we the grass did tread,
　　Or sit us down to talk.

'Twas all in vain to look around,
    Alas! she was not there;   50
Oh, Death has hid her from my sight,
    She does not charm my ear.

I went and viewed that room once more,
    Where my dear parent lay,
When Death with solemn tidings came   55
    To take her life away.

Here did I see her jawbone fall,
    And then her eye-strings break;
And, just before, I thought she strove
    These words to me to speak: 60

'Oh, Hannah, put your trust in God';
    And could she then foresee
The train of troubles that did come
    Upon unhappy me?

What could a dying mother say   65
    More to a daughter dear,
Than bid her put her trust in God,
    A friend that's ever near?

Again I was in that doleful room,
    When thus to me 'twas said: 70
'Your father you'll alive not see' –
    I cried, 'What! is he dead?'

As if in frenzy, scarce believed
    What they to me did say;
But oh! indeed, he dropped down dead –   75
    'Twas on a market day.

Why do I wound my heart afresh?
    These sorrows are too keen:
Then stop, my muse, and turn, my thoughts,
    Unto a pleasing theme.   80

For all that ever died in Christ
 Shall meet him in the air;
So grand, so sweet, so fine a sight!
 I hope I shall be there.

Oh, talk not of a birthday night,   85
 Nor coronation day;
Compared, they lose their beauties all,
 When saints shall come away.

With palms of victory in their hands,
 And crowns upon each head;   90
And loud hosannas will proclaim
 His praise, that once was dead.

Rejoice, ye saints, he lives anew;
 Your Judge is now your King;
Sweet alleluias all will cry,   95
 And endless praises sing.

HELEN LEIGH

The Natural Child

Let not the title of my verse offend,
 Nor let the prude contract her rigid brow;
That helpless innocence demands a friend,
 Virtue herself will cheerfully allow:

And should my pencil prove too weak to paint   5
 The ills attendant on the babe ere born,
Whose parents swerved from Virtue's mild restraint,
 Forgive the attempt, nor treat the muse with scorn.

Yon rural farm, where mirth was wont to dwell,
 Of melancholy now appears the seat;   10
Solemn and silent as the hermit's cell –
 Say what, my muse, has caused a change so great?

This hapless morn an infant first saw light,
  Whose innocence a better fate might claim
Than to be shunned as hateful to the sight,   15
  And banished soon as it receives a name.

No joy attends its entrance into life,
  No smile upon its mother's face appears.
She cannot smile, alas! she is no wife,
  But vents the sorrow of her heart in tears.   20

No father flies to clasp it to his breast,
  And bless the power that gave it to his arms;
To see his form, in miniature expressed,
  Or trace, with ecstasy, its mother's charms.

Unhappy babe! thy father is thy foe!   25
  Oft shall he wish thee numbered with the dead;
His crime entails on thee a load of woe,
  And sorrow heaps on thy devoted head.

Torn from its mother's breast, by shame or pride –
  No matter which – to hireling hands assigned;   30
A parent's tenderness when thus denied,
  Can it be thought its nurse is over-kind?

Too many like this infant we may see,
  Exposed, abandoned, helpless and forlorn;
Till death, misfortune's friend, has set them free   35
  From a rude world which gave them nought but scorn.

Too many mothers – horrid to relate!
  Soon as their infants breathe the vital air,
Deaf to their plaintive cries, their helpless state,
  Led on by shame, and driven by despair,   40

Fell murderers become – Here cease, my pen,
  And leave these wretched victims of despair;
But ah! what punishments await the men
  Who, in such depths of misery, plunge the fair?

WILLIAM BLAKE

The Little Boy Found

The little boy lost in the lonely fen,
Led by the wandering light,
Began to cry; but God, ever nigh,
Appeared like his father in white.

He kissed the child, and by the hand led,   5
And to his mother brought,
Who in sorrow pale, through the lonely dale,
Her little boy weeping sought.

The Land of Dreams

'Awake, awake, my little boy,
Thou wast thy mother's only joy;
Why dost thou weep in thy gentle sleep?
Awake! thy father does thee keep.'

'Oh, what land is the land of dreams?   5
What are its mountains and what are its streams?
Oh, father, I saw my mother there,
Among the lilies by waters fair.

'Among the lambs, clothed in white,
She walked with her Thomas in sweet delight.   10
I wept for joy, like a dove I mourn;
Oh, when shall I again return?'

'Dear child, I also by pleasant streams
Have wandered all night in the land of dreams;

But though calm and warm the waters wide,   15
I could not get to the other side.'

'Father, O father, what do we here
In this land of unbelief and fear?
The land of dreams is better far,
Above the light of the morning star.'   20

HENRIETTA O'NEILL

Written on Seeing Her Two Sons at Play

Sweet age of blest illusion! blooming boys,
Ah, revel long in childhood's thoughtless joys
With light and pliant spirits, that can stoop
To follow, sportively, the rolling hoop;
To watch the sleeping top with gay delight,   5
Or mark, with raptured gaze, the sailing kite;
Or, eagerly pursuing Pleasure's call,
Can find it centred on the bounding ball!
Alas! the day will come when sports like these
Must lose their magic and their power to please: 10
Too swiftly fled, the rosy hours of youth
Shall yield their fairy charms to mournful truth.
Even now a mother's fond prophetic fear
Sees the dark train of human ills appear;
Views various fortune for each lovely child,   15
Storms for the bold, and anguish for the mild;
Beholds already those expressive eyes
Beam a sad certainty of future sighs;
And dreads each suffering those dear breasts may know
In their long passage through a world of woe,   20
Perchance predestined every pang to prove,
That treacherous friends inflict, or faithless love.
For, ah! how few have found existence sweet,
Where grief is sure, but happiness deceit!

ISABELLA KELLY

To an Unborn Infant

Be still, sweet babe, no harm shall reach thee,
   Nor hurt thy yet unfinished form;
Thy mother's frame shall safely guard thee
   From this bleak, this beating storm.

Promised hope! expected treasure!   5
   Oh, how welcome to these arms!
Feeble, yet they'll fondly clasp thee,
   Shield thee from the least alarms.

Loved already, little blessing,
   Kindly cherished, though unknown,   10
Fancy forms thee sweet and lovely,
   Emblem of the rose unblown.

Though thy father is imprisoned,
   Wronged, forgotten, robbed of right,
I'll repress the rising anguish,   15
   Till thine eyes behold the light.

Start not, babe! the hour approaches
   That presents the gift of life;
Soon, too soon, thou'lt taste of sorrow
   In these realms of care and strife.   20

Share not thou a mother's feelings,
   Hope vouchsafes a pitying ray;
Though a gloom obscures the morning,
   Bright may shine the rising day.

Live, sweet babe, to bless thy father,   25
   When thy mother slumbers low;

Slowly lisp her name that loved him,
   Through a world of varied woe.

Learn, my child, the mournful story
   Of thy suffering mother's life;   30
Let thy father not forget her
   In a future, happier wife.

Babe of fondest expectation,
   Watch his wishes in his face;
What pleased in me may'st thou inherit,   35
   And supply my vacant place.

Whisper all the anguished moments
   That have wrung this anxious breast:
Say, I lived to give thee being,
   And retire to endless rest.   40

JOANNA BAILLIE

from A Winter's Day

  The family cares call next upon the wife
To quit her mean but comfortable bed.
And first she stirs the fire and blows the flame,
Then from her heap of sticks, for winter stored,
An armful brings; loud-crackling as they burn,   5
Thick fly the red sparks upward to the roof,
While slowly mounts the smoke in wreathy clouds.
On goes the seething pot with morning cheer,
For which some little wishful hearts await,
Who, peeping from the bedclothes, spy well-pleased   10
The cheery light that blazes on the wall,
And bawl for leave to rise. –
Their busy mother knows not where to turn,
Her morning work comes now so thick upon her.
One she must help to tie his little coat,   15

Unpin his cap, and seek another's shoe.
When all is o'er, out to the door they run,
With new-combed sleeky hair and glistening cheeks,
Each with some little project in his head . . .

A Mother to Her Waking Infant

Now in thy dazzling half-oped eye,
Thy curled nose and lip awry,
Thy up-hoist arm and nodding head,
And little chin with crystal spread,
Poor helpless thing! what do I see,   5
    That I should sing of thee?

From thy poor tongue no accents come,
Which can but rub thy toothless gum;
Small understanding boasts thy face,
Thy shapeless limbs nor step nor grace;   10
A few short words thy feats may tell,
    And yet I love thee well.

When sudden wakes the bitter shriek,
And redder swells thy little cheek;
When rattled keys thy woes beguile,   15
And through the wet eye gleams the smile,
Still for thy weakly self is spent
    Thy silly little plaint.

But when thy friends are in distress,
Thou'lt laugh and chuckle ne'er the less,   20
Nor e'en with sympathy be smitten,
Though all are sad but thee and kitten.
Yet, little varlet that thou art,
    Thou twitchest at the heart.

Thy rosy cheeks so soft and warm;   25
Thy pinky hand and dimpled arm;

Thy silken locks that scantly peep,
With gold-tipped ends, where circles deep
Around thy neck in harmless grace
So soft and sleekly hold their place,   30
Might harder hearts with kindness fill,
    And gain our right good will.

Each passing clown bestows his blessing,
Thy mouth is worn with old wives' kissing:
E'en lighter looks the gloomy eye   35
Of surly sense, when thou art by;
And yet I think whoe'er they be,
    They love thee not like me.

Perhaps when time shall add a few
Short years to thee, thou'lt love me too.   40
Then wilt thou through life's weary way
Become my sure and cheering stay:
Wilt care for me, and be my hold,
    When I am weak and old.

Thou'lt listen to my lengthened tale,   45
And pity me when I am frail –
But see, the sweepy spinning fly
Upon the window takes thine eye.
Go to thy little senseless play –
    Thou dost not heed my lay.   50

ANON

On My Own Little Daughter, Four Years Old

Sweet lovely infant, innocently gay,
    With blooming face arrayed in peaceful smiles,
How light thy cheerful heart doth sportive play,
    Unconscious of all future cares and toils.

With what delight I've seen thy little feet   5
   Dancing with pleasure at my near approach!
Eager they ran my well-known form to meet,
   Secure of welcome, fearless of reproach.

Then happy hast thou prattled in mine ear
   Thy little anxious tales of pain or joy;   10
Thy fears lest faithful Tray thy frock should tear,
   Thy pride when ladies give the gilded toy.

How oft, when sad reflection dimmed mine eye,
   As memory recalled past scenes of woe,
Thy tender heart hath heaved the expressive sigh   15
   Of sympathy, for ills thou could'st not know.

Oft too in silence I've admired that face,
   Beaming with pity for a mother's grief,
Whilst in each anxious feature I could trace
   Compassion eager to afford relief.   20

E'en now methinks I hear the artless tongue,
   Lisping sweet sounds of comfort to mine ear:
'Oh, fret no more – your Fanny is not gone –
   She will not go – don't cry – your Fanny's here.'

If, ere her mind attains its full-grown strength,   25
   Thy will consigns me to an early tomb,
If in Thy sight my thread's near run its length
   And called by Thee I cannot watch her bloom –

O heavenly Father, guard my infant child;
   Protect her steps through this wide scene of care;   30
Within her breast implant each virtue mild,
   And teach her all she ought to hope or fear.

WILLIAM WORDSWORTH

The Sailor's Mother

One morning (raw it was, and wet –
A foggy day in winter time)
A woman on the road I met,
Not old, though something past her prime:
Majestic in her person, tall and straight;   5
And like a Roman matron's was her mien and gait.

The ancient spirit is not dead;
Old times, thought I, are breathing there;
Proud was I that my country bred
Such strength, a dignity so fair.   10
She begged an alms, like one in poor estate;
I looked at her again, nor did my pride abate.

When from these lofty thoughts I woke,
'What is it,' said I, 'that you bear
Beneath the covert of your cloak,   15
Protected from this cold, damp air?'
She answered, soon as she the question heard,
'A simple burden, sir, a little singing-bird'.

And, thus continuing, she said:
'I had a son who, many a day   20
Sailed on the seas, but he is dead:
In Denmark he was cast away,
And I have travelled weary miles to see
If aught which he had owned might still remain for me.

'The bird and cage they both were his: 25
'Twas my son's bird; and neat and trim
He kept it: many voyages
The singing-bird had gone with him;
When last he sailed he left the bird behind,
From bodings, as might be, that hung upon his mind.   30

'He to a fellow lodger's care
Had left it, to be watched and fed,
And pipe its song in safety; – there
I found it when my son was dead;
And now, God help me for my little wit,   35
I bear it with me, sir – he took so much delight in it'.

The Cottager to Her Infant

The days are cold, the nights are long,
The north-wind sings a doleful song;
Then hush again upon my breast;
All merry things are now at rest,
      Save thee, my pretty love!   5

The kitten sleeps upon the hearth,
The crickets long have ceased their mirth;
There's nothing stirring in the house
Save one wee, hungry, nibbling mouse,
      Then why so busy thou?   10

Nay, start not at that sparkling light;
'Tis but the moon that shines so bright
On the window pane bedropped with rain:
Then, little darling, sleep again,
      And wake when it is day.   15

Confirmation Continued

I saw a mother's eye intensely bent
Upon a maiden trembling as she knelt,
In and for whom the pious mother felt
Things that we judge of by a light too faint:
Tell, if ye may, some star-crowned muse or saint,   5

Tell what rushed in, from what she was relieved,
Then, when her child the hallowing touch received,
And such vibration through the mother went
That tears burst forth amain. Did gleams appear?
Opened a vision of that blissful place   10
Where dwells a sister-child? And was power given
Part of her lost one's glory back to trace
Even to this rite? For thus she knelt, and, ere
The summer leaf had faded, passed to heaven.

MARY TIGHE

Sonnet Addressed to My Mother

O thou, whose tender smile most partially
  Hath ever blessed thy child – to thee belong
  The graces which adorn my first wild song,
If aught of grace it knows, nor thou deny
Thine ever-prompt attention to supply.   5
  But let me lead thy willing ear along
  Where virtuous love still bids the strain prolong
His innocent applause since, from thine eye,
  The beams of love first charmed my infant breast,
And from thy lip Attention's soothing voice   10
  That eloquence of tenderness expressed,
Which still my grateful heart confessed divine –
Oh ever may its accents sweet rejoice
The soul which loves to own whate'er it has is thine!

SAMUEL TAYLOR COLERIDGE

Sonnet

TO A FRIEND WHO ASKED ME HOW IT FELT WHEN THE NURSE FIRST PRESENTED MY INFANT TO ME

Charles! my slow heart was only sad when first
    I scanned that face of feeble infancy:
For dimly on my thoughtful spirit burst
    All I had been, and all my child might be!
But when I saw it on its mother's arm,   5
    And hanging at her bosom (she the while
    Bent o'er its features with a tearful smile)
Then I was thrilled and melted, and most warm
Impressed a father's kiss: and all beguiled
    Of dark remembrance and presageful fear,   10
    I seemed to see an angel-form appear –
'Twas even thine, beloved woman mild!
    So for the mother's sake the child was dear,
And dearer was the mother for the child.

A Child's Evening Prayer

Ere on my bed my limbs I lay,
God grant me peace my prayers to say:
O God! preserve my mother dear
In strength and health for many a year;
And, O! preserve my father too,   5
And may I pay him reverence due;
And may I my best thoughts employ
To be my parents' hope and joy;
And O! preserve my brothers both
From evil doings and from sloth,   10

And may we always love each other,
Our friends, our father, and our mother:
And still, O Lord, to me impart
An innocent and grateful heart,
That after my great sleep I may   15
Awake to thy eternal day! Amen.

'The Singing Kettle and the Purring Cat'

The singing kettle and the purring cat,
The gentle breathing of the cradled babe,
The silence of the mother's love-bright eye,
And tender smile answering its smile of sleep.

THOMAS MOORE

To My Mother

Written in a Pocket-Book, 1822

They tell us of an Indian tree
    Which, howsoe'er the sun and sky
May tempt its boughs to wander free,
    And shoot and blossom, wide and high,
Far better loves to bend its arms   5
    Downward again to that dear earth
From which the life, that fills and warms
    Its grateful being, first had birth.

'Tis thus, though wooed by flattering friends,
    And fed with fame (*if* fame it be),   10
This heart, my own dear mother, bends,
    With love's true instinct, to thee.

FELICIA HEMANS

To My Mother

If e'er for human bliss or woe
I feel the sympathetic glow;
If e'er my heart has learned to know
      The generous wish or prayer;
Who sowed the germ, with tender hand?   5
Who marked its infant leaves expand?
      My mother's fostering care.

And if *one* flower of charms refined
May grace the garden of my mind,
      'Twas she who nursed it there;   10
   She loved to cherish and adorn
      Each blossom of the soil;
   To banish every weed and thorn,
      That oft opposed her toil.

And, oh! if e'er I've sighed to claim   15
The palm, the living palm of fame,
      The glowing wreath of praise;
If e'er I've wished the glittering stores
That fortune on her favourite pours,
'Twas but that wealth and fame, if mine,   20
Round *thee*, with streaming rays might shine,
      And gild thy sun-bright days.

Yet not that splendour, pomp, and power,
Might then irradiate every hour;
For these, my mother, well I know,   25
On thee no rapture could bestow;
But could thy bounty, warm and kind,
Be, like thy wishes, unconfined,
And fall, as manna from the skies,
And bid a train of blessings rise,   30

             Diffusing joy and peace;
The tear-drop, grateful, pure and bright,
For thee would beam with softer light
Than all the diamond's crystal rays,
Than all the emerald's lucid blaze;   35
And joys of heaven would thrill thy heart,
To bid one bosom-grief depart,
              One tear, one sorrow cease!

Then, oh! may heaven, that loves to bless,
Bestow the power to cheer distress;   40
Make thee its minister below,
To light the cloudy path of woe;
To visit the deserted cell
Where indigence is doomed to dwell;
To raise, when drooping to the earth,   45
The blossoms of neglected worth;
And round, with liberal hand, dispense
The sunshine of beneficence.

But ah, if fate should still deny
Delights like these, too rich and high;   50
If grief and pain thy steps assail
In life's remote and wintry vale;
Then, as the wild Aeolian lyre
      Complains with soft, entrancing number
When the loud storm awakes the wire,   55
      And bids enchantment cease to slumber;
So filial love, with soothing voice,
E'en then shall teach me to rejoice:
E'en then shall sweeter, milder sound,
When sorrow's tempest raves around;   60
While dark misfortune's gales destroy
The frail mimosa-buds of hope and joy!

CAROLINE CLIVE

The Mother

I feel within myself a life
That holds 'gainst death a feeble strife;
They say 'tis destined that the womb
Shall be its birthplace and its tomb.
O child! if it be so, and thou   5
Thy native world must never know,
Thy mother's tears will mourn the day
   When she must kiss thy Death-born face.
But oh! how lightly thou wilt pay
   The forfeit due from Adam's race!   10
Thou wilt have lived, but not have wept,
   Have died, and yet have known no pain;
And sin's dark presence will have swept
   Across thy soul, and left no stain.
Mine is thy life; my breath, thy breath: 15
   I only feel the dread, the woe;
And in thy sickness or thy death,
   Thy mother bears the pain, not thou.

Life nothing means for thee, but still
It is a living thing, I feel;   20
A sex, a shape, a growth are thine,
A form, a human face divine;
A heart with passions wrapped therein,
A nature doomed, alas, to sin;
A mind endowed with latent fire,   25
To glow, unfold, expand, aspire;
Some likeness from thy father caught,
Or by remoter kindred taught;
Some faultiness of mind or frame,
To wake the bitter sense of shame;   30
Some noble passions to unroll,
   The generous deed, the human tear;

Some feeling which thy mother's soul
   Has poured on thine, while dwelling near.
All this must pass unbloomed away   35
   To worlds remote from earthly day;
Worlds whither we, by paths less brief,
Are journeying on through joy and grief,
And where thy mother, now forlorn,
May learn to know her child unborn;   40
Oh, yes! created thing, I trust
Thou too wilt rise with Adam's dust.

CHARLES SWAIN

A Mother's Love

There's beauty in the breath of morn,
   When earth is bright with dew and light,
When summer buds and flowers are born –
   And clouds seem angels on their flight!
There's joy which innocence imparts,   5
   A sweetness every breast may prove;
But what's so sweet to human hearts,
   So precious, as a mother's love?

The sun to light the east may fail,
   The morn forsake her fields of dew,   10
The silvery clouds forget to sail
   Along their sea of heavenly blue;
And all that's bright may pass away –
   Our hopes recall, our friends remove,
Yet, constant, 'midst a world's decay,   15
   Still sweet would be a mother's love.

The Widowed Mother

She sat beside the abbey gate, –
   The sun was setting fast;
Its light played in her baby's face!
   Her own was overcast!
'Oh, smile not here, my baby dear!   5
   Smile not while I deplore,
And seek relief in tears of grief,
   For him who is no more!'

The clouds lay turning to the west
   Their gold and crimson rim;   10
And still – as if the babe they blest –
   Threw golden smiles on him!
'Oh, change that brow, my baby, now,
   Or turn thy gaze from me;
I cannot bear, 'midst all my care,   15
   Thy little smiles to see!

'Some pity take for his dear sake,
   Who loved thee whilst he'd breath;
And told thee this with his last kiss,
   And clung to thee in death!'   20
But still that ray in golden play
   Around the baby crept;
And still 'twould smile, though all the while
   The widowed mother wept.

WILLIAM BARNES

The Mother's Dream

I'd a dream tonight
   As I vell asleep –
Oh! the touchen zight

  Still do mëake me weep, –
Ov my little bwoy   5
That's a-took awoy;
Aye, about my joy
  I wer not to keep.

As in heaven high
  I my child did seek,   10
There, in traïn, come by
  Childern feäir an' meek;
Each in lilywhite,
Wi' a lamp alight;
Each wer clear to zight,   15
  But noo words did speak.

Then a-looken sad
  Come my child in turn;
But the lamp he had,
  Oh! he didden burn;   20
He, to clear my doubt,
Zaid, a-turn'd about,
Your tears put en out;
  Mother, never murn.

WINTHROP MACKWORTH PRAED

Mater Desiderata

I cannot guess her face or form;
  But what to me is form or face?
I do not ask the weary worm
  To give me back each buried grace
Of glistening eyes or trailing tresses.   5
  I only feel that she is here,
    And that we meet, and that we part;
  And that I drink within mine ear,

And that I clasp around my heart
Her sweet still voice and soft caresses.   10

Not in the waking thought by day,
  Nor in the sightless dream by night,
Do the mild tones and glances play
  Of her who was my cradle's light!
But in some twilight of calm weather   15
  She glides by fancy dimly wrought,
    A glittering cloud, a darkling beam,
  With all the quiet of a thought
    And all the passion of a dream
Link'd in a golden spell together.   20

SARA COLERIDGE

The Mother

Full oft beside some gorgeous fane
  The youngling heifer bleeds and dies;
Her life-blood issuing forth amain,
  While wreaths of incense climb the skies.

The mother wanders all around,   5
  Thro' shadowy groves and lightsome glade;
Her footmarks on the yielding ground
  Will prove what anxious quest she made.

The stall where late her darling lay
  She visits oft with eager look;   10
In restless movements wastes the day,
  And fills with cries each neighb'ring nook.

She roams along the willowy copse,
  Where purest waters softly gleam;
But ne'er a leaf or blade she crops,   15
  Nor couches by the gliding stream.

No youthful kine, tho' fresh and fair,
   Her vainly searching eyes engage;
No pleasant fields relieve her care,
   No murmuring streams her grief assuage.   20

THOMAS AIRD

My Mother's Grave

Oh rise, and sit in soft attire!
Wait but to know my soul's desire!
I'd call thee back to earthly days,
To cheer thee in a thousand ways!
Ask but this heart for monument,   5
And mine shall be a large content!

A crown of brightest stars to thee!
How did thy spirit wait for me,
And nurse thy waning light, in faith
That I would stand 'twixt thee and death!   10
Then tarry on thy bowing shore,
Till I have asked thy sorrows o'er!

I came not, and I cry to save
Thy life from the forgetful grave
One day, that I may well declare   15
How I have thought of all thy care,
And love thee more than I have done,
And make thy days with gladness run.

I'd tell thee where my youth has been,
Of perils past, of glories seen;   20
I'd tell thee all my youth has done,
And ask of things to choose and shun;
And smile at all thy needless fears,
But bow before thy solemn tears.

Come, walk with me, and see fair earth,   25
And men's glad ways, and join their mirth!
Ah me! is this a bitter jest?
What right have I to break thy rest?
Well hast thou done thy worldly task,
Nothing hast thou of me to ask.   30

Men wonder till I pass away,
They think not but of useless clay:
Alas for Age, that this should be!
But I have other thoughts of thee;
And I would wade thy dusty grave,   35
To kiss the head I cannot save.

Oh for life's power, that I might see
Thy visage swelling to be free!
Come near, oh burst that earthly cloud,
And meet me, meet me, lowly bowed!   40
Alas! in corded stiffness pent,
Darkly I guess thy lineament.

I might have lived, thou still on earth,
Like one to thee of alien birth,
Mother; but now that thou art gone,   45
I feel as in the world alone:
The wind which lifts the streaming tree,
The skies seem cold and strange to me:

I feel a hand untwist the chain
Of all thy love, with shivering pain,   50
From round my heart: this bosom's bare,
And less than wonted life is there.
Ay, well indeed it may be so!
And well for thee my tears may flow!

Because that I of thee was part,   55
Made of the blood-drops of thy heart;
My birth I from thy body drew,
And I upon thy bosom grew;
Thy life was set my life upon;
And I was thine, and not my own.   60

Because I know there is not one
To think of me as thou hast done,
From morn till star-light, year by year;
For me thy smile repaid thy tear;
And fears for me, and no reproof,   65
When once I dared to stand aloof!

My punishment, that I was far
When God unloosed thy weary star!
My name was in thy faintest breath,
And I was in thy dream of death;   70
And well I know what raised thy head,
When came the mourner's muffled tread!

Alas! I cannot tell thee now
I could not come to hold thy brow.
And wealth is late, nor aught I've won   75
Were worth to hear thee call thy son
In that dark hour when bands remove,
And none are named but names of love.

Alas for me, I missed that hour!
My hands for this shall miss their power;   80
For thee, the sun, and dew, and rain,
Shall ne'er unbind thy grave again,
Nor let thee up the light to see,
Nor let thee up to be with me!

Yet sweet thy rest from care and strife,   85
And many pains that hurt thy life!
Turn to thy God – and blame thy son –
To give thee more than I have done:
Thou God, with joy beyond all years,
Fill up the channels of her tears! –   90

Thou car'st not now for soft attire,
Yet wilt thou hear my soul's desire;
To earth I dare not call thee more,
But speak from off thy awful shore:
Oh ask this heart for monument,   95
And mine shall be a large content!

ELIZABETH BARRETT BROWNING

from **Aurora Leigh, Book 1**

I, writing thus, am still what men call young;
I have not so far left the coasts of life
To travel inward, that I cannot hear
That murmur of the outer Infinite
Which unweaned babies smile at in their sleep   5
When wondered at for smiling; not so far,
But still I catch my mother at her post
Beside the nursery door, with finger up,
'Hush, hush – here's too much noise!' while her sweet
    eyes
Leap forward, taking part against her word   10
In the child's riot. Still I sit and feel
My father's slow hand, when she had left us both,
Stroke out my childish curls across his knee,
And hear Assunta's daily jest (she knew
He liked it better than a better jest)   15
Inquire how many golden scudi went
To make such ringlets. O my father's hand,
Stroke heavily, heavily the poor hair down,
Draw, press the child's head closer to thy knee!
I'm still too young, too young, to sit alone.   20

I write. My mother was a Florentine,
Whose rare blue eyes were shut from seeing me
When scarcely I was four years old, my life
A poor spark snatched up from a failing lamp
Which went out therefore. She was weak and frail;   25
She could not bear the joy of giving life,
The mother's rapture slew her. If her kiss
Had left a longer weight upon my lips
It might have steadied the uneasy breath,
And reconciled and fraternised my soul   30
With the new order. As it was, indeed,

I felt a mother-want about the world,
And still went seeking, like a bleating lamb
Left out at night in shutting up the fold, –
As restless as a nest-deserted bird   35
Grown chill through something being away, though
    what
It knows not. I, Aurora Leigh, was born
To make my father sadder, and myself
Not overjoyous, truly. Women know
The way to rear up children (to be just),   40
They know a simple, merry, tender knack
Of tying sashes, fitting baby-shoes,
And stringing pretty words that make no sense,
And kissing full sense into empty words,
Which things are corals to cut life upon,   45
Although such trifles: children learn by such,
Love's holy earnest in a pretty play
And get not over-early solemnised,
But seeing, as in a rose-bush, Love Divine
Which burns and hurts not, – not a single bloom, –   50
Become aware and unafraid of Love.
Such good do mothers. Fathers love as well
– Mine did, I know, – but still with heavier brains,
And wills more consciously responsible,
And not as wisely, since less foolishly;   55
So mothers have God's licence to be missed . . .

from **Isobel's Child**

To rest the weary nurse has gone:
        An eight day watch watched she,
    Still rocking beneath sun and moon
        The baby on her knee,
    Till Isobel its mother said   5
    'The fever waneth – wend to bed,
    For now the watch comes round to me.'

Then wearily the nurse did throw
    Her pallet in the darkest place
Of that sick room, and slept and dreamed: 10
    For, as the gusty wind did blow
        The night-lamp's flare across her face,
She saw, or seemed to see, but dreamed,
    That the poplars tall on the opposite hill,
The seven tall poplars on the hill,   15
Did clasp the setting sun until
His rays dropped from him, pined and still
    As blossoms in frost,
Till he waned and paled, so weirdly crossed,
To the colour of moonlight which doth pass   20
Over the dank ridged churchyard grass.
The poplars held the sun, and he
The eyes of the nurse that they should not see
– Not for a moment, the babe on her knee,
Though she shuddered to feel that it grew to be   25
Too chill, and lay too heavily.

She only dreamed; for all the while
    'Twas Lady Isobel that kept
        The little baby: and it slept
Fast, warm, as if its mother's smile,   30
Laden with love's dewy weight,
And red as rose of Harpocrate,
Dropped upon its eyelids, pressed
Lashes to cheek in a sealed rest.

And more and more smiled Isobel   35
To see the baby sleep so well –
She knew not that she smiled.
Against the lattice, dull and wild
Drive the heavy, droning drops,
    Drop by drop, the sound being one;   40
As momently time's segments fall
On the ear of God, who hears through all
    Eternity's unbroken monotone:
And more and more smiled Isobel
To see the baby sleep so well –   45

She knew not that she smiled.
The wind in intermission stops
  Down in the beechen forest,
    Then cries aloud
As one at the sorest, 50
    Self-stung, self-driven,
And rises up to its very tops,
Stiffening erect the branches bowed,
  Dilating with a tempest-soul
The trees that with their dark hands break 55
Through their own outline, and heavy roll
  Shadows as massive as clouds in heaven
    Across the castle lake.
And more and more smiled Isobel
To see the baby sleep so well; 60
She knew not that she smiled;
She knew not that the storm was wild;
Through the uproar drear she could not hear
The castle clock which struck anear –
She heard the low, light breathing of her child. 65

O sight for wondering look!
While the external nature broke
Into such abandonment,
While the very mist, heart-rent
By the lightning, seemed to eddy 70
Against nature, with a din, –
A sense of silence and of steady
Natural calm appeared to come
From things without, and enter in
The human creature's room. 75

So motionless she sate,
  The babe asleep upon her knees,
You might have dreamed their souls had gone
Away to things inanimate,
In such to live, in such to moan; 80
And that their bodies had ta'en back,
  In mystic change, all silences
That cross the sky in cloudy rack,

Or dwell beneath the reedy ground
In waters safe from their own sound: 85
        Only she wore
The deepening smile I named before,
And *that* a deepening love expressed;
And who at once can love and rest?

In sooth the smile that then was keeping   90
Watch upon the baby sleeping,
    Floated with its tender light
Downward, from the drooping eyes,
Upward, from the lips apart,
    Over cheeks which had grown white   95
With an eight-day weeping:
All smiles come in such a wise
    Where tears shall fall or have of old –
Like northern lights that fill the heart
    Of heaven in sign of cold.   100

Motionless she sate.
Her hair had fallen by its weight
On each side of her smile and lay
Very blackly on the arm
Where the baby nestled warm,   105
Pale as baby carved in stone
Seen by glimpses of the moon
    Up a dark cathedral aisle:
But, through the storm, no moonbeam fell
Upon the child of Isobel –   110
Perhaps you saw it by the ray
    Alone of her still smile. . . .

ALFRED, LORD TENNYSON

The Grandmother

And Willy, my eldest born, is gone, you say, little Anne?
Ruddy and white, and strong on his legs, he looks like a
  man.
And Willy's wife has written: she never was over-wise,
Never the wife for Willy: he wouldn't take my advice.

For, Annie, you see, her father was not the man to save,   5
Hadn't a head to manage, and drank himself into his grave.
Pretty enough, very pretty! But I was against it for one,
Eh! – but he wouldn't hear me – and Willy, you say, is
  gone.

Willy, my beauty, my eldest-born, the flower of the flock;
Never a man could fling him: for Willy stood like a rock.   10
'Here's a leg for a babe of a week!' says doctor; and he
  would be bound,
There was not his like that year in twenty parishes round.

Strong of his hands, and strong on his legs, but still of his
  tongue!
I ought to have gone before him: I wonder he went so
  young.
I cannot cry for him, Annie: I have not long to stay;   15
Perhaps I shall see him the sooner, for he lived far away.

Why do you look at me, Annie? You think I am hard and
  cold;
But all my children have gone before me, I am so old:
I cannot weep for Willy, nor can I weep for the rest;
Only at your age, Annie, I could have wept with the best.   20

For I remember a quarrel I had with your father, my dear,
All for a slanderous story, that dost me many a tear.

I mean your grandfather, Annie: it cost me a world of woe,
Seventy years ago, my darling, seventy years ago.

For Jenny, my cousin, had come to the place, and I knew
  right well   25
That Jenny had tripped in her time: I knew, but would not
  tell.
And she to be coming and slandering me, the base little
  liar!
But the tongue is a fire as you know, my dear, the tongue
  is a fire.

And the parson made it his text that week, and he said
  likewise,
That a lie which is half a truth is ever the blackest of lies,   30
That a lie which is all a lie may be met and fought with
  outright,
But a lie which is part a truth is a harder matter to fight.

And Willy had not been down to the farm for a week and
  a day;
And all things looked half-dead, though it was the middle
  of May.
Jenny, to slander me, who knew what Jenny had been!   35
But soiling another, Annie, will never make oneself clean.

And I cried myself well-nigh blind, and all of an evening
  late
I climbed to the top of the garth, and stood by the road at
  the gate.
The moon like a rick on fire was rising over the dale,
And whit, whit, whit, in the bush beside me chirruped the
  nightingale.   40

All of a sudden he stopped: there passed by the gate of the
  farm
Willy – he didn't see me – and Jenny hung on his arm.
Out into the road I started, and spoke I scarce knew how;
Ah, there's no fool like the old one – it makes me angry
  now.

Willy stood up like a man, and looked the thing that he
    meant;   45
Jenny, the viper, made me a mocking curtsey and went.
And I said, 'Let us part: in a hundred years it'll all be the
    same,
You cannot love me at all, if you love not my good name.'

And he turned, and I saw his eyes all wet, in the sweet
    moonshine:
'Sweetheart, I love you so well that your good name is
    mine.   50
And what do I care for Jane, let her speak of you well or
    ill;
But marry me out of hand: we two will be happy still.'

'Marry you, Willy!' said I, 'but I needs must speak my
    mind,
And I fear you'll listen to tales, be jealous, and hard, and
    unkind.'
But he turned and clasped me in his arms, and answered,
    'No, love, no';   55
Seventy years ago, my darling, seventy years ago.

So Willy and I were wedded: I wore a lilac gown;
And the ringers rang with a will, and he gave the ringers
    a crown.
But the first that ever I bare was dead before he was born,
Shadow and shine is life, little Annie, flower and thorn.   60

That was the first time, too, that ever I thought of death.
There lay the sweet little body that never had drawn a
    breath.
I had not wept, little Anne, not since I had been a wife;
But I wept like a child that day, for the babe had fought
    for his life.

His dear little face was troubled, as if with anger or pain: 65
I looked at the still little body – his trouble had all been in
    vain.
For Willy I cannot weep, I shall see him another morn:

But I wept like a child for the child that was dead before
   he was born.

But he cheered me, my good man, for he seldom said me
   nay:
Kind, like a man, was he; like a man, too, would have his
   way: 70
Never jealous – not he: we had many a happy year;
And he died, and I could not weep – my own time seemed
   so near.

But I wished it had been God's will that I, too, then could
   have died:
I began to be tired a little, and fain had slept at his side.
And that was ten years back, or more, if I don't forget: 75
But as to the children, Annie, they're all about me yet.

Pattering over the boards, my Annie who left me at two,
Pattering she goes, my own little Annie, an Annie like
   you:
Pattering over the boards, she comes and goes at her will,
While Harry is in the five-acre and Charlie ploughing the
   hill.   80

And Harry and Charlie, I hear them too – they sing to
   their team:
Often they come to the door in a pleasant kind of a dream.
They come and sit by my chair, they hover about my
   bed –
I am not always certain if they be alive or dead.

And yet I know for a truth, there's none of them left alive;   85
For Harry went at sixty, your father at sixty-five:
And Willy, my eldest-born, at nigh threescore and ten;
I knew them all as babies, and now they're elderly men.

For mine is a time of peace, it is not often I grieve;
I am oftener sitting at home in my father's farm at eve;   90
And the neighbours come and laugh and gossip, and so
   do I;

I find myself often laughing at things that have long gone
   by.

To be sure the preacher says, our sins should make us sad:
But mine is a time of peace, and there is grace to be had;
And God, not man, is the Judge of us all when life shall
   cease;   95
And in this Book, little Annie, the message is one of peace.

And age is a time of peace, so it be free from pain,
And happy has been my life; but I would not live it again.
I seem to be tired a little, that's all, and long for rest;
Only at your age, Annie, I could have wept with the best.   100

So Willy has gone, my beauty, my eldest-born, my flower;
But how can I weep for Willy, he has but gone for an
   hour –
Gone for a minute, my son, from this room into the next;
I, too, shall go in a minute. What time have I to be vexed?

And Willy's wife has written, she never was over-wise.   105
Get me my glasses, Annie: thank God that I keep my eyes.
There is but a trifle left you, when I shall have passed
   away.
But stay with the old woman now: you cannot have long
   to stay.

from **Demeter and Persephone (In Enna)**

   So in this pleasant vale we stand again,
The field of Enna, now once more ablaze
With flowers that brighten as thy footstep falls,
All flowers – but for one black blur of earth
Left by that closing chasm, through which the car   5
Of dark Aidoneus rising rapt thee hence.
And here, my child, though folded in thine arms,
I feel the deathless heart of motherhood

Within me shudder, lest the naked glebe
Should yawn once more into the gulf, and thence   10
The shrilly whinnyings of the team of Hell,
Ascending, pierce the glad and songful air,
And all at once their arched necks, midnight-maned,
Jet upward through the mid-day blossom. No!
For, see, thy foot has touched it; all the space   15
Of blank earth-baldness clothes itself afresh,
And breaks into the crocus-purple hour
That saw thee vanish.

             Child, when thou wert gone,
I envied human wives, and nested birds,
Yea, the cubbed lioness; went in search of thee   20
Through many a palace, many a cot, and gave
Thy breast to ailing infants in the night,
And set the mother waking in amaze
To find her sick one whole; and forth again
Among the wail of midnight winds, and cried,   25
'Where is my loved one? Wherefore do ye wail?
And out from all the night an answer shrilled,
'We know not, and we know not why we wail.'
I climbed on all the cliffs of all the seas,
And asked the waves that moan about the world   30
'Where? do ye make your moanings for my child?'
And round from all the world the voices came
'We know not, and we know not why we moan.'
'Where?' and I stared from every eagle-peak,
I thridded the black heart of all the woods,   35
I peered through tomb and cave, and in the storms
Of Autumn swept across the city, and heard
The murmur of their temples chanting me,
Me, me, the desolate Mother! 'Where?' – and turned,
And fled by many a waste, forlorn of man,   40
And grieved for man through all my grief for thee, –
The jungle rooted in his shattered hearth,
The serpent coiled about his broken shaft,
The scorpion crawling over naked skulls; –
I saw the tiger in the ruined fane   45
Spring from his fallen god, but trace of thee
I saw not; and far on, and, following out

A league of labyrinthine darkness, came
On three grey heads beneath a gleaming rift.
'Where?' and I heard one voice from all the three   50
'We know not, for we spin the lives of men,
And not of gods, and know not why we spin!
There is a fate beyond us.' Nothing knew . . .

'Remembering Him Who Waits Thee Far Away'

Remembering him who waits thee far away,
And with thee, Mother, taught us first to pray,
Accept on this your golden bridal day
     The Book of Prayer.

JEAN INGELOW

Seven Times Seven: Longing for Home

    A song of a boat: –
  There was once a boat on a billow:
  Lightly she rocked to her port remote,
And the foam was white in her wake like snow,
And her frail mast bowed when the breeze would blow   5
    And bent like a wand of willow.

  I shaded mine eyes one day when a boat
    Went curtseying over the billow,
  I marked her course till a dancing mote
She faded out on the moonlit foam,   10
And I stayed behind in the dear loved home;
    And my thoughts all day were about the boat
      And my dreams upon the pillow.

I pray you hear my song of a boat,
  For it is but short: –   15
My boat, you shall find none fairer afloat,
  In river or port.
Long I looked out for the lad she bore,
  On the open desolate sea,
And I think he sailed to the heavenly shore, 20
  For he came not back to me –
      Ah me!

   A song of a nest: –
 There was once a nest in a hollow:
Down in the mosses and knot-grass pressed, 25
 Soft and warm, and full to the brim –
 Vetches leaned over it, purple and dim,
  With buttercup buds to follow.

I pray you hear my song of a nest,
  For it is not long: –   30
You shall never light, in a summer quest
  The bushes among –
Shall never light on a prouder sitter,
  A fairer nestful, nor ever know
A softer sound than their tender twitter, 35
  That wind-like did come and go.

  I had a nestful once of my own,
    Ah happy, happy I!
Right dearly I loved them: but when they were grown
    They spread out their wings to fly – 40
  O, one after one they flew away
    Far up to the heavenly blue,
  To the better country, the upper day,
    And – I wish I was going too.

  I pray you, what is the nest to me, 45
    My empty nest?
  And what is the shore where I stood to see
    My boat sail down to the west?
  Can I call that home where I anchor yet,

Though my good man has sailed? 50
Can I call that home where my nest was set,
  Now all its hope hath failed?
Nay, but the port where my sailor went,
  And the land where my nestlings be:
There is the home where my thoughts are sent, 55
  The only home for me –
                    Ah me!

FREDERICK LOCKER-LAMPSON

A Terrible Infant

I recollect a nurse call'd Ann
  Who carried me about the grass,
And one fine day a fine young man
  Came up, and kiss'd the pretty lass.
She did not make the least objection! 5
        Thinks I, 'Aha!
  When I can talk I'll tell Mamma.'
– And that's my earliest recollection.

To My Grandmother

(Suggested by a Picture by Mr Romney)

This relative of mine
Was she seventy and nine
  When she died?
By the canvas may be seen
How she looked at seventeen, 5
  As a bride.

Beneath a summer tree
As she sits, her reverie
  Has a charm;
Her ringlets are in taste, –   10
What an arm! and what a waist
  For an arm!

In bridal coronet,
Lace, ribbons, and *coquette*
  Falbala;   15
Were Romney's limning true,
What a lucky dog were you,
  Grandpapa!

Her lips were sweet as love, –
They are parting! Do they move?   20
  Are they dumb? –
Her eyes are blue, and beam
Beseechingly, and seem
  To say, 'Come.'

What funny fancy slips   25
From atween these cherry lips?
  Whisper me,
Sweet deity, in paint,
What canon says I mayn't
  Marry thee?   30

That good-for-nothing Time
Has a confidence sublime!
  When I first
Saw this lady, in my youth,
Her winters had, forsooth,   35
  Done their worst.

Her locks (as white as snow)
Once shamed the swarthy crow;
  By and by
That fowl's avenging sprite   40
Set his cloven hoof for spite
  In her eye.

Her rounded form was lean,
And her silk was bombazine: –
    Well I wot,   45
With her needles would she sit,
And for hours would she knit, –
    Would she not?

Ah, perishable clay!
Her charms had dropp'd away   50
    One by one.
But if she heaved a sigh
With a burthen, it was 'Thy
    Will be done.'

In travail, as in tears,   55
With the fardel of her years
    Overprest, –
In mercy was she borne
Where the weary ones and worn
    Are at rest.   60

I'm fain to meet you there, –
If as witching as you were,
    Grandmamma!
This nether world agrees
That the better it must please   65
    Grandpapa.

COVENTRY PATMORE

The Toys

My little Son, who look'd from thoughtful eyes
And moved and spoke in quiet grown-up wise,
Having my law the seventh time disobey'd,
I struck him, and dismiss'd
With hard words and unkiss'd,   5

His Mother, who was patient, being dead.
Then, fearing lest his grief should hinder sleep,
I visited his bed,
But found him slumbering deep,
With darken'd eyelids, and their lashes yet   10
From his late sobbing wet.
And I, with moan,
Kissing away his tears, left others of my own;
For, on a table drawn beside his head,
He had put, within his reach,   15
A box of counters and a red-vein'd stone,
A piece of glass abraded by the beach
And six or seven shells,
A bottle with bluebells,
And two French copper coins, ranged here with careful
    art,   20
To comfort his sad heart.
So when that night I pray'd
To God, I wept, and said:
Ah, when at last we lie with tranced breath,
Not vexing Thee in death,   25
And Thou rememberest of what toys
We made our joys,
How weakly understood,
Thy great commanded good,
Then, fatherly not less   30
Than I whom Thou hast moulded from the clay,
Thou'lt leave Thy wrath, and say,
'I will be sorry for their childishness.'

CHARLES STUART CALVERLEY

Waiting

'O come, O come,' the mother pray'd
    And hush'd her babe: 'let me behold
Once more thy stately form array'd
    Like autumn woods in green and gold!

'I see thy brethren come and go;   5
   Thy peers in stature, and in hue
Thy rivals. Some like monarchs glow
   With richest purple: some are blue

'As skies that tempt the swallow back;
   Or red as, seen o'er wintry seas,   10
The star of storm; or barr'd with black
   And yellow, like the April bees.

'Come they and go! I heed not, I.
   Yet others hail their advent, cling
All trustful to their side, and fly   15
   Safe in their gentle piloting

'To happy homes on heath or hill,
   By park or river. Still I wait
And peer into the darkness: still
   Thou com'st not – I am desolate.   20

'Hush! hark! I see a towering form!
   From the dim distance slowly roll'd
It rocks like lilies in a storm,
   And O, its hues are green and gold:

'It comes, it comes! Ah rest is sweet,   25
   And there is rest, my babe, for us!'
She ceased, as at her very feet
   Stopp'd the St John's Wood omnibus.

Motherhood

She laid it where the sunbeams fall
Unscann'd upon the broken wall.
Without a tear, without a groan,
She laid it near a mighty stone,
Which some rude swain had haply cast   5

Thither in sport, long ages past,
And Time with mosses had o'erlaid,
And fenced with many a tall grass blade,
And all about bid roses bloom
And violets shed their soft perfume.   10
There, in its cool and quiet bed,
She set her burden down and fled:
Nor flung, all eager to escape,
One glance upon the perfect shape
That lay, still warm and fresh and fair,   15
But motionless and soundless there.

No human eye had mark'd her pass
Across the linden-shadow'd grass
Ere yet the minster clock chimed seven:
Only the innocent bird of heaven –   20
The magpie, and the rook whose nest
Swings as the elm tree waves his crest –
And the lithe cricket, and the hoar
And huge-limb'd hound that guards the door,
Look'd on when, as a summer wind   25
That, passing, leaves no trace behind,
All unapparell'd, barefoot all,
She ran to that old ruin'd wall,
To leave upon the chill dank earth
(For ah! she never knew its worth)   30
'Mid hemlock rank, and fern and ling,
And dews of night, that precious thing.

And there it might have lain forlorn
From morn till eve, from eve to morn:
But that, by some wild impulse led,   35
The mother, ere she turn'd and fled,
One moment stood erect and high;
Then pour'd into the silent sky
A cry so jubilant, so strange,
That Alice – as she strove to range   40
Her rebel ringlets at her glass –
Sprang up and gazed across the grass;
Shook back those curls so fair to see,

Clapp'd her soft hands in childish glee;
And shriek'd – her sweet face all aglow,   45
    Her very limbs with rapture shaking –
    'My hen has laid an egg, I know;
    And only hear the noise she's making!'

On the Brink

I watch'd her as she stooped to pluck
    A wildflower in her hair to twine;
And wish'd that it had been my luck
    To call her mine.

Anon I heard her rate with mad   5
    Mad words her babe within its cot;
And felt particularly glad
    That it had not.

I knew (such subtle brains have men)
    That she was uttering what she shouldn't;   10
And thought that I would chide, and then
    I thought I wouldn't:

Who could have gazed upon that face,
    Those pouting coral lips, and chided?
A Rhadamanthus, in my place,   15
    Had done as I did:

For ire wherewith our bosoms glow
    Is chain'd there oft by Beauty's spell;
And, more than that, I did not know
    The widow well.   20

So the harsh phrase pass'd unreproved.
    Still mute – (O brothers, was it sin?) –
I drank, unutterably moved,
    Her beauty in:

And to myself I murmur'd low,   25
   As on her upturn'd face and dress
The moonlight fell, 'Would she say No,
   By chance, or Yes?'

She stood so calm, so like a ghost
   Betwixt me and that magic moon,   30
That I already was almost
   A finish'd coon.

But when she caught adroitly up
   And sooth'd with smiles her little daughter;
And gave it, if I'm right, a sup   35
   Of barley-water;

And, crooning still the strange sweet lore
   Which only mothers' tongues can utter,
Snow'd with deft hand the sugar o'er
   Its bread-and-butter;   40

And kiss'd it clingingly – (Ah, why
   Don't women do these things in private?) –
I felt that if I lost her, I
   Should not survive it:

And from my mouth the words nigh flew –   45
   The past, the future, I forgat 'em:
'Oh! if you'd kiss me as you do
   That thankless atom!'

But this thought came ere I spake,
   And froze the sentence on my lips: 50
'They err who marry wives that make
   Those little slips.'

It came like some familiar rhyme,
   Some copy to my boyhood set;
And that's perhaps the reason I'm   55
   Unmarried yet.

Would she have own'd how pleased she was,
    And told her love with widow's pride?
I never found that out, because
    I never tried.   60

Be kind to babes and beasts and birds:
    Hearts may be hard, though lips are coral;
And angry words are angry words:
    And that's the moral.

JOSEPH SKIPSEY

'Mother Wept, and Father Sigh'd'

Mother wept, and father sigh'd;
    With delight aglow
Cried the lad, 'Tomorrow,' cried,
    'To the pit I go.'

Up and down the place he sped, –   5
    Greeted old and young;
Far and wide the tidings spread;
    Clapt his hands and sung.

Came his cronies; some to gaze
    Wrapp'd in wonder; some   10
Free with counsel; some with praise;
    Some with envy dumb.

'May he,' many a gossip cried,
    'Be from peril kept.'
Father hid his face and sigh'd,   15
    Mother turn'd and wept.

ELLEN JOHNSTON

A Mother's Love

I love thee, I love thee, and life will depart
Ere thy mother forget thee, sweet child of her heart;
Yea, death's shadows only my memory can dim,
For thou'rt dearer than life to me – Mary Achin.

I love thee, I love thee, and six years hath now fled   5
Since first on my bosom I pillowed thy head;
Since I first did behold thee in sorrow and sin,
Thou sweet offspring of false love – my Mary Achin.

I love thee, I love thee, and twelve months hath now past,
My sweet child, since I gazed on thy fairy form last;   10
And our parting brought sorrow, known only to Him
Who can see through the heart's depths – my Mary Achin.

I love thee, I love thee, oh! when shalt thou rest
Thy sweet angel face on this heart-baring breast;
Thy last parting kiss lingers still on my chin,   15
Embalmed with a blessing from Mary Achin.

I love thee, I love thee, thy beauty and youth
Are spotless and pure as the fountain of truth;
Thou'rt my star in the night till daybreak begin,
And my sunshine by noontide – my Mary Achin.

I love thee, I love thee, wherever I go
Thou'rt shrined in my bosom in joy or in woe;
A murmuring music my fancy doth win,
'Tis the voice of my darling – Mary Achin.

I love thee, I love thee, is ever my lay,
I sigh it by night and I sing it by day;
Its chorus swells forth like the stern patriot's hymn,
Thrice hallowed with visions of Mary Achin.

I love thee, I love thee, though now far away
Thou'rt nearer and dearer to me every day;
Would they give me my choice – a nation to win –
I would not exchange with my Mary Achin.

THOMAS HARDY

News for Her Mother

One mile more is
Where your door is,
   Mother mine! –
Harvest's coming,
Mills are strumming,   5
   Apples fine,
And the cider made to-year will be as wine.

Yet, not viewing
What's a-doing
   Here around   10
Is it thrills me,
And so fills me
   That I bound
Like a ball or leaf or lamb along the ground.

Tremble not now   15
At your lot now,
   Silly soul!
Hosts have sped them
Quick to wed them,
   Great and small,   20
Since the first two sighing half-hearts made a whole.

Yet I wonder,
Will it sunder
   Her from me?
Will she guess that   25

I said 'Yes,' – that
   His I'd be,
Ere I thought she might not see him as I see!

Old brown gable,
Granary, stable,   30
   Here you are!
O my mother,
Can another
   Ever bar
Mine from my heart, make thy nearness seem afar?   35

The Christening

Whose child is this they bring
   Into the aisle? –
At so superb a thing
The congregation smile
And turn their heads awhile.   5

Its eyes are blue and bright,
   Its cheeks like rose;
Its simple robes unite
Whitest of calicoes
With lawn, and satin bows.   10

A pride in the human race
   At this paragon
Of mortals, lights each face
While the old rite goes on;
But ah, they are shocked anon.   15

What girl is she who peeps
   From the gallery stair,
Smiles palely, redly weeps,
With feverish furtive air
As though not fitly there?   20

'I am the baby's mother;
    This gem of the race
The decent fain would smother,
And for my deep disgrace
I am bidden to leave the place.'   25

'Where is the baby's father?' –
    'In the woods afar.
He says there is none he'd rather
Meet under moon or star
Than me, of all that are.   30

'To clasp me in lovelike weather,
    Wish fixing when,
He says: To be together
At will, just now and then,
Makes him the blest of men;   35

'But chained and doomed for life
    To slovening
As vulgar man and wife,
He says, is another thing:
Yea, sweet Love's sepulchring!'   40

In Childbed

    In the middle of the night
Mother's spirit came and spoke to me,
    Looking weariful and white –
As 'twere untimely news she broke to me.

    'O my daughter, joyed are you   5
To own the weetless child you mother there;
    "Men may search the wide world through,"
You think, "nor find so fair another there!"

    'Dear, this midnight time unwombs
Thousands just as rare and beautiful;   10

Thousands whom High Heaven foredooms
To be as bright, as good, as dutiful.

'Source of ecstatic hopes and fears
And innocent maternal vanity,
    Your fond exploit but shapes for tears   15
New thoroughfares in sad humanity.

'Yet as you dream, so dreamt I
When life stretched forth its morning ray to me;
    Other views for by and by!' . . .
Such strange things did my mother say to me.   20

ALICE MEYNELL

The Modern Mother

    Oh, what a kiss
With filial passion overcharged is this!
    To this misgiving breast
This child runs, as a child ne'er ran to rest
Upon the light heart and the unoppressed.   5

    Unhoped, unsought!
A little tenderness this mother thought
    The utmost of her meed.
She looked for gratitude; content indeed
With thus much that her nine years' love had bought.   10

    Nay, even with less.
This mother, giver of life, death, peace, distress,
    Desired, ah! not so much
Thanks as forgiveness; and the passing touch
Expected, and the slight, the brief caress.   15

    O filial light
Strong in these childish eyes, these new, these bright

Intelligible stars! Their rays
Are near the constant earth, guides in the maze,
Natural, true, keen in this dusk of days.   20

Maternity

One wept whose only child was dead,
　　New-born, ten years ago.
'Weep not; he is in bliss,' they said.
　　She answered, 'Even so,

'Ten years ago was born in pain   5
　　A child, not now forlorn.
But oh, ten years ago, in vain,
　　A mother, a mother was born.'

The Girl on the Land

　'When have I known a boy
Kinder than this my daughter, or his kiss
More filial, or the clasping of his joy
　　Closer than this?'

　Thus did a mother think;   5
And yet her daughter had been long away,
Estranged, on other business; but the link
　　Was fast today.

　This mother, who was she?
I know she was the earth, she was the land.   10
Her daughter, a gay girl, toiled happily,
　　Sheaves in hand.

ROBERT LOUIS STEVENSON

To Alison Cunningham
From Her Boy

For the long nights you lay awake
And watched for my unworthy sake:
For your most comfortable hand
That led me through the uneven land:
For all the story-books you read: 5
For all the pains you comforted:
For all you pitied, all you bore,
In sad and happy days of yore: –
My second mother, my first wife,
The angel of my infant life –   10
From the sick child, now well and old,
Take, nurse, the little book you hold!

And grant it, heaven, that all who read
May find as dear a nurse at need,
And every child who lists my rhyme,   15
In the bright, fireside, nursery clime,
May hear it in as kind a voice
As made my childish days rejoice!

To My Mother

You too, my mother, read my rhymes
For love of unforgotten times,
And you may chance to hear once more
The little feet along the floor.

To Any Reader

As from the house your mother sees
You playing round the garden trees,
So you may see, if you will look
Through the windows of this book,
Another child, far, far away,   5
And in another garden, play.
But do not think you can at all,
By knocking on the window, call
That child to hear you. He intent
Is all on his play-business bent.   10
He does not hear; he will not look,
Nor yet be lured out of this book.
For, long ago, the truth to say,
He has grown up and gone away,
And it is but a child of air   15
That lingers in the garden there.

EDITH NESBIT

Song

Oh, baby, baby, baby dear,
We lie alone together here;
The snowy gown and cap and sheet
With lavender are fresh and sweet;
Through half-closed blinds the roses peer   5
To see and love you, baby dear.

You are so tired, we like to lie
Just doing nothing, you and I,
Within the darkened quiet room.
The sun sends dusk rays through the gloom,   10
Which is no gloom since you are here,
My little life, my baby dear.

Soft sleepy mouth so vaguely pressed
Against your new-made mother's breast.
Soft little hands in mine I fold,   15
Soft little feet I kiss and hold,
Round soft smooth head and tiny ear,
All mine, my own, my baby dear.

And he we love is far away!
But he will come some happy day,   20
You need but me, and I can rest
At peace with you beside me pressed.
There are no questions, longings vain,
No murmurings, no doubt, nor pain,
Only content and we are here,   25
      My baby dear.

FRANCIS THOMPSON

'Little Jesus'

Little Jesus, wast Thou shy
Once, and just as small as I?
And what did it feel like to be
Out of heaven, and just like me?
Didst Thou sometimes think of *there*,   5
And ask where all the angels were?
I should think that I would cry
For my house all made of sky;
I would look about the air,
And wonder where my angels were;   10
And at waking 'twould distress me –
Not an angel there to dress me!
Hadst Thou ever any toys,
Like us little girls and boys?
And didst Thou play in heaven with all   15
The angels that were not too tall,
With stars for marbles? Did the things

Play *Can you see me?* through their wings?
And did Thy mother let Thee spoil
Thy robes, with playing on *our* soil?   20
How nice to have them always new
In heaven, because 'twas quite clean blue!

Didst Thou kneel at night to pray,
And didst Thou join Thy hands, this way?
And did they tire sometimes, being young,   25
And make the prayers seem very long?
And dost Thou like it best, that we
Should join our hands to pray to Thee?
I used to think, before I knew,
The prayer not said unless we do.   30
And did Thy mother at the night
Kiss Thee, and fold the clothes in right?
And didst Thou feel quite good in bed,
Kiss'd, and sweet, and Thy prayers said?

Thou canst not have forgotten all   35
That it feels like to be small:
And Thou know'st I cannot pray
To Thee in my father's way –
When Thou wast so little, say,
Couldst Thou talk Thy Father's way? –   40

So, a little Child, come down
And hear a child's tongue like Thy own;
Take me by the hand and walk,
And listen to my baby-talk.
To Thy Father show my prayer   45
(He will look, Thou art so fair),
And say: 'O Father, I, Thy Son,
Bring the prayer of a little one.'

And He will smile, that children's tongue
Has not changed since Thou wast young!   50

JOHN MASEFIELD

To His Mother, C.L.M.

In the dark womb where I began
My mother's life made me a man.
Through all the months of human birth
Her beauty fed my common earth.
I cannot see, nor breathe, nor stir,   5
But through the death of some of her.

Down in the darkness of the grave
She cannot see the life she gave.
For all her love, she cannot tell
Whether I use it ill or well,   10
Nor knock at dusty doors to find
Her beauty dusty in the mind.

If the grave's gates could be undone,
She would not know her little son,
I am so grown. If we should meet,   15
She would pass by me in the street,
Unless my soul's face let her see
My sense of what she did for me.

What have I done to keep in mind
My debt to her and womankind?   20
What woman's happier life repays
Her for those months of wretched days?
For all my mouthless body leech'd
Ere Birth's releasing hell was reach'd?

What have I done, or tried, or said   25
In thanks to that dear woman dead?
Men triumph over women still,
Men trample women's rights at will,
And man's lust roves the world untamed.

*   *   *

O grave, keep shut lest I be shamed!   30

LILIAN BOWES LYON

A Son

A middle-aged farm-labourer lived here,
And loved his wife; paid rent to hard eternity
Six barren years, till thorn-tree blessed she bore
A son with a bird's glint, and wheat-straw hair.
Sweet life! Yet neither boasted.   5
The boy was a tassel flown by gaunt serenity,
Hedge banner in the September of the War.

A jettisoned bomb fell; at noonday there,
Where take my dusty oath a cottage stood.
Great with unspendable centuries of maternity,   10
'At least he had struck seven,' she said, 'this year – '
Of different grace; of blood.
The man looks bent; yet neither girds at God,
Remembering it was beautiful while it lasted.

ANON

The Death of Queen Jane

Queen Jane lay in labour full nine days or more,
Till the women were so tired, they could stay no longer
   there.

'Good women, good women, good women as ye be,
Do open my right side, and find my baby.'

'Oh no,' said the women, 'that never may be,   5
We will send for King Henry and hear what he say.'

King Henry was sent for, King Henry did come:
'What do ail you, my lady, your eyes look so dim?'

'King Henry, King Henry, will you do one thing for me?
That's to open my right side, and find my baby.'   10

'Oh no,' said King Henry, 'that's a thing I'll never do.
If I lose the flower of England, I shall lose the branch too.'

King Henry went mourning, and so did his men,
And so did the dear baby, for Queen Jane did die then.

And how deep was the mourning, how black were the
    bands,
How yellow, yellow were the flamboys they carried in their   15
    hands.

There was fiddling, aye, and dancing on the day the babe
    was born,
But poor Queen Jane beloved lay as cold as a stone.

ANON

Whistle, Daughter, Whistle

'O mother, I longs to get married,
I longs to be a bride.
I longs to lay with that young man
And close to by his side,
Oh happy should I be,   5
For I'm young and merry and almost weary
Of my virginity.'

'O daughter, I was twenty
Before that I was wed
And many a long and lonesome mile   10
I carried my maidenhead.'

'O mother, that may be,
It's not the case by me,
For I'm young and merry and almost weary
Of my virginity.'   15

'Daughter, daughter, whistle,
And you shall have a sheep.'
'I cannot whistle, mother,
But I can sadly weep.
My maidenhead does grieve me,   20
That fills my heart with fear.
It is a burden, a heavy burden,
It's more than I can bear.'

'Daughter, daughter, whistle,
And you shall have a cow.'   25
'I cannot whistle, mother,
For 'deed I don't know how.
My maidenhead does grieve me,
That fills my heart with fear.
It is a burden, a heavy burden,   30
It's more than I can bear.'

'Daughter, daughter, whistle,
And you shall have a man.'
          (*whistles*)
'You see very well I can.'
'You nasty, impudent Jane,   35
I'll pull your courage down.
Take off your silks and satins,
Put on your working gown.
I'll send you to the fields,
A-tossing of the hay   40
With your fork and rake the hay to make
And then hear what you say.'

'Mother, don't be so cruel
To send me to the fields
Where young men may entice me   45
And to them I may yield.

For mother, it's quite well known
I am not too young grown,
For it is a pity a maid so pretty
As I should lay alone.'   50

ANON

The Cruel Mother

There was a lady lived in York
   All alone and a loney,
A farmer's son he courted her,
   All down by the greenwood sidey.

He courted her for seven long years,   5
At last she proved with child by him.

She pitched her knee against a tree,
And there she found great misery.

She pitched her back against a thorn,
And there she had her baby born.   10

She drew the fillet off her head,
And bound the baby's hands and legs.

She drew a knife both long and sharp,
She pierced the baby's innocent heart.

She wiped the knife upon the grass,   15
The more she wiped the blood run fast.

She washed her hands all in the spring,
Thinking to turn a maid again.

As she was going to her father's hall,
She saw three babes a-playing at ball.   20

One dressed in silk, the other in satin,
The other stark-naked as ever was born.

'O dear baby, if you was mine,
I'd dress you in silk and satins so fine.'

'O dear mother, I once was thine,   25
You never would dress me, coarse or fine.

'The coldest earth it was my bed,
The green grass was my coverlet.

'O mother, mother, for your sin,
Heaven gate you shall not enter in.   30

'There is a fire beyond hell's gate,
And there you'll burn both early and late.'

ANON

'Where Have You Been All Day'

'Where have you been all day, Henry my son,
Where have you been all day, my beloved one?'
'In the fields, dear mother, in the fields, dear mother,
Make my bed for I'm afraid in my heart,
And I want to lie down.'   5

'Where did you see your father, Henry my son,
Where did you see your father, my beloved one?'
'In the fields, dear mother, in the fields, dear mother,
Make my bed for I'm afraid in my heart,
And I want to lie down.'   10

'What did your father give you, Henry my son,
What did your father give you, my beloved one?'
'Water, dear mother, water, dear mother,
Make my bed for I'm afraid in my heart,
And I want to lie down.'   15

'What shall I give your father, Henry my son,
What shall I give your father, my beloved one?'
'A rope to hang him, a rope to hang him,
Make my bed for I'm afraid in my heart,
And I want to lie down.'   20

'Where shall I make your bed, Henry my son,
Where shall I make your bed, my beloved one?'
'In the churchyard, dear mother, in the churchyard, dear
   mother,
Make my bed for I'm afraid in my heart,
And I want to lie down.'   25

'How shall I make your bed, Henry my son,
How shall I make your bed, my beloved one?'
'Long and narrow, long and narrow,
Make my bed for I'm afraid in my heart,
And I want to lie down – for ever.'   30

ANON

'All Under the Leaves'

All under the leaves, the leaves of life,
I met with virgins seven,
And one of them was Mary mild,
Our Lord's mother from heaven.

'Oh what are you seeking, you seven fair maids,   5
All under the leaves of life?
Come tell, come tell me what seek you
All under the leaves of life?'

'We're seeking for no leaves, Thomas,
But for a friend of thine;   10
We're seeking for sweet Jesus Christ,
To be our guide and thine.'

'Go you down, go you down to yonder town,
And sit in the gallery;
And there you'll find sweet Jesus Christ,   15
Nailed to a big yew-tree.'

So down they went to yonder town,
As fast as foot could fall,
And many a grievous bitter tear
From the virgins' eyes did fall.   20

'Oh peace, mother, oh peace, mother,
Your weeping doth me grieve;
Oh I must suffer this,' He said,
'For Adam and for Eve.'

'Oh how can I my weeping leave   25
Or my sorrows undergo,
Whilst I do see my own son die,
When sons I have no mo'?'

'Dear mother, dear mother, you must take John,
All for to be your son,   30
And he will comfort you sometimes,
Mother, as I have done.'

'Oh come, thou John Evangelist,
Thou'rt welcome unto me,
But more welcome my own dear son,   35
That I nursed upon my knee.'

Then He laid His head on His right shoulder,
Seeing death it struck Him nigh:
'The Holy Ghost be with your soul –
I die, mother dear, I die.'   40

Oh the rose, the rose, the gentle rose,
And the fennel that grows so green!
God give us grace in every place
To pray for our king and queen.

Furthermore, for our enemies all   45
Our prayers they should be strong.
Amen, Good Lord, your charity
Is the ending of my song.

ANNE RIDLER

For a Child Expected

Lovers whose lifted hands are candles in winter,
Whose gentle ways like streams in the easy summer,
Lying together
For secret setting of a child, love what they do,
Thinking they make that candle immortal, those streams
   forever flow,   5
And yet do better than they know.

So the first flutter of a baby felt in the womb,
Its little signal and promise of riches to come,
Is taken in its father's name;
Its life is the body of his love, like his caress,   10
First delicate and strange, that daily use
Makes dearer and priceless.

Our baby was to be the living sign of our joy,
Restore to each the other's lost infancy;
To a painter's pillaging eye   15
Poet's coiled hearing, add the heart we might earn
By the help of love; all that our passion would yield
We put to planning our child.

The world flowed in; whatever we liked we took:
For its hair, the gold curls of the November oak   20
We saw on our walk;
Snowberries that make a Milky Way in the wood
For its tender hands; calm screen of the frozen flood
For our care of its childhood.

But the birth of a child is an uncontrollable glory;   25
Cat's cradle of hopes will hold no living baby,
Long though it lay quietly.
And when our baby stirs and struggles to be born
It compels humility: what we began
Is now its own.   30

For *as the sun that shines through glass*
So Jesus in His Mother was.
Therefore every human creature,
Since it shares in His nature,
In candle-gold passion or white   35
Sharp star should show its own way of light.
May no paternal dread or dream
Darken our darling's early beam:
May she grow to her right powers
Unperturbed by passion of ours.   40

GEORGE BARKER

To My Mother

Most near, most dear, most loved and most far,
Under the window where I often found her
Sitting as huge as Asia, seismic with laughter,
Gin and chicken helpless in her Irish hand,
Irresistible as Rabelais, but most tender for   5
The lame dogs and hurt birds that surround her, –
She is a procession no one can follow after
But be like a little dog following a brass band.

She will not glance up at the bomber, or condescend
To drop her gin and scuttle to a cellar,   10
But lean on the mahogany table like a mountain
Whom only faith can move, and so I send
O all my faith and all my love to tell her
That she will move from mourning into morning.

ELIZABETH JENNINGS

To My Mother at 73

Will you always catch me unaware,
Find me fumbling, holding back? You claim
Little, ask ordinary things, don't dare
Utter endearments much but speak my name
As if you hoped to find a child there,   5
There on the phone, the same

You tried to quiet. You seem to want the years
Wrapped up and tossed away. You need me to
Prove you are needed. Can you sense the tears
So pent up, so afraid of hurting you?   10
Must we both fumble not to show our fears
Of holding back our pain, our kindness too?

Notes

John Audelay, fifteenth century

'The Mother of Mary':   Bodleian Library, Oxford, MS Douce 302. This is a carol for the feast of St Anne, mother of the Virgin Mary, 26 July, a feast of obligation since the late fourteenth century. Her life was narrated in the apocryphal Book of James. Her husband was St **Joachim** (l.18). The refrain, printed at the beginning, follows each verse. **1 may:** maid. **5 leech:** healer. **7 Herefore:** therefore (the refrain follows). **8 gladded:** made glad. **15 forlore:** doomed to destruction; given to sin. **18 Fore:** previously. **25 root ... Jesse:** Isaiah 11:1; **cleped:** called. **29 at my weeting:** to my knowledge. **36 into ... dignity:** as successor to. **43** *Mater ... Filium*: Mother, pray to your Son (Latin). **44 outlere:** exile. **45–6** *Nobis ... fine*: give us joy without end (Latin).

James Ryman, fl. c. 1492

'Meekly We Sing and Say to Thee':   Cambridge University Library MS Ee. 1. 12. A petition to Mary, as mother of Christ, to intercede on behalf of fallen humanity, the offspring of mother Eve. **2** *Maria ... salue*: Mary, our hope, greetings (Latin). **26 laud:** praise. **32 of:** through. **40 city:** the New Jerusalem (Revelation 21–2).

Anon, fifteenth century

'Noel, el, el, el, el, el, el ...':   British Library MS Sloane 2593. The carol begins with the Annunciation, 25 March (see **Anon, 'What, Heard Ye Not?' headnote**, below). **2 greet with:** greeted by. **5 ground:** earth. **6** *Gabriel nuntio:* Gabriel being the messenger (Latin, as are the phrases that follow). **10** *Cum ... lilio:* by the lily of modesty (the lily is an emblem of Mary's virginity). **14** *Fulget resurrectio:* [His] resurrection

NOTES

blazes forth. **18** *Motu . . . proprio*: borne by His own desire (or impulse).
20 styest: ascend; **wone**: dwell. **22** *In . . . palatio*: in the heavenly temple.

Anon, fifteenth century

'Mary Mother, Come and See':   British Library MS Sloane 2593. A carol
on the Passion. **4 woe**: pain, sorrow, grief. **19 rood**: cross. **21–2 Woman
. . . sake**: John 19:25–7. **27 wight**: person, creature.

Anon, sixteenth century

'What, Heard Ye Not?':   Balliol College, Oxford MS 354. On the Annun-
ciation, following Luke 1:26–38. **4 avail**: aid. **17 Thy . . . fain**: Your
words bring great joy to me. **20** *Te Deum*: the Latin canticle of praise
from Matins, attributed to St Ambrose, '*Te Deum laudamus*' ('We praise
Thee, O God').

Anon, 1560s?

'Flower of Roses, Angels' Joy':   from *The Arundel Harington Manuscript of
Tudor Poetry*, ed. Ruth Hughey (Columbus, Ohio: Ohio State University
Press, 1960), vol. I. A poem to the Virgin Mary based on images from the
Litany of Our Lady (mystical rose, Tower of David, etc.). **2 Noy**: Noah,
whose ark was an emblem of salvation (Genesis 6–8). **4 sprite**: spirit.
9 used: accustomed. **12 clouts**: clothes.

Richard Edwards, c. 1523–66

Amantium Irae Amoris Redintegratio: from *The Paradise of Dainty
Devices*, ed. Richard Edwards (1576). **Title**: Latin; translated as the refrain.
1 my . . . bed: in night clothes to my bed. **33 perdy**: indeed (literally, by
God; from the French).

Arthur Golding, translator, c. 1536–c. 1605

[The Punishment of Niobe]: from Ovid, *Metamorphoses* (1565–7), Book VI. Title: **Niobe:** one of the archetypal mothers, along with Eve, Mary, Venus (see **Creech**, below) and Demeter (see **Tennyson**, below). Wife of Amphion, king of Thebes, by whom she had seven daughters and seven sons, she was so proud of her offspring that she boasted that she was superior as a mother to Latona, who had borne only two children, Phoebus Apollo, the sun god, and Diana, goddess of the moon and hunting. Apollo and Diana took umbrage on their mother's behalf and slew all Niobe's children, who remained unburied for nine days. Their grieving mother was turned to stone, but still felt her grief. **3 tho:** then. **11 mo:** more. **18 weed:** clothes. **21 ghost:** spirit. **24 blin:** cease. **32 wrying her:** twisting herself. **36 quite:** utterly. **38 waxed:** grew. **44 forewent:** passed away.

Edmund Spenser, c. 1552–99

[Charissa]: from *The Fairy Queen* (1590), Book I, canto 10, stanzas 29–32. Title: **Charissa:** Charity was traditionally depicted as a suckling mother with a number of babies; the **yellow** and **doves** signify marriage and Venus, goddess of love (and see **Creech**, below); her **tiara** recalls Charity's usual crown of flames and the gold crown of virtue. **1 By this:** by this time. **3 unacquainted:** unknown to her. **4 freshest:** most blooming. **5 bounty rare:** extreme goodness. **6 personage:** appearance. **7 compare:** equal. **14 joyed:** it rejoiced. **16 still:** ever. **18 ouches:** brooches. **19 passing price:** surpassing value; **uneath:** scarcely. **22 fair:** courteously. **24 requites:** repays; **seeming meet:** fitting.

Nicholas Breton, c. 1555–1626

A Sweet Lullaby: from *The Arbour of Amorous Devices* (1597). **1 silly:** defenceless; weak. **3 I doubt:** I'm afraid; **dole:** sorrow. **15 smart:** affliction.

John Harington, d. 1582

To His Mother: first published 1769; text from Ruth Hughey, *John Harington of Stepney: Tudor Gentleman. His Life and Works* (Columbus, Ohio: Ohio State University Press, 1971). **9 strait:** tight spot.

Robert Greene, 1558–92

'Weep Not, My Wanton': from Menaphon (1589). **1 wanton:** term of affection.

Emilia Lanier, c. 1569–1645

[A Defence of Eve]: from *Salve Deus Rex Judaeorum* [Hail, God, King of the Jews: Latin] (1611). The trial of Christ before Pilate is found in all the gospels. **1 cause:** case. **4 woeful bands:** grievous bonds. **27 bereaved:** deprived. **28 condescended:** given way. **31 alleged:** quoted. **32 That . . . wise:** Genesis 3:3–6. **43 strait:** with specific limits. **59 prove:** experience. **69 train:** deceit.

Ben Jonson, 1572–1637

Epigram 22: On My First Daughter: from *Epigrams*, in *Works* (1616).

Epigram 62: To Fine Lady Would-be: from *Epigrams*, in *Works* (1616).

William Browne of Tavistock, c. 1590–c. 1645

[Epitaph]: first published 1623. Text: *Poems* (1895). The subject of the poem is Mary Sidney, Countess of Pembroke (1561–1621), poet and translator, sister of Sir Philip Sidney, who married Henry Herbert, second Earl of Pembroke, in 1577. **1 hearse:** framework over tomb; funeral pall. **10 Niobe:** see **Arthur Golding, Title note** above.

Robert Herrick, 1591–1674

To Dianeme. A Ceremony in Gloucester: from *Hesperides* (1648). **1 simnel:** rich currant cake eaten on Mid-Lent Sunday. As this was also Mothering Sunday, simnel cake was, in addition, brought as a gift by children to their mothers.

Francis Quarles, 1592–1644

On the Infancy of Our Saviour: from *Divine Fancies* (1632). **16 kiss:** that of Judas (e.g., Matthew 26:47–9). **20 weed:** piece of clothing.

Rachel Speight, 1597–?

From **The Dream:** from *Mortality's Memorandum, with a Dream Prefixed* (1621). **9 Tophet:** hell. **10 Canaan:** God's promised land (Genesis 17:8). **28 lenify:** mitigate. **30 smart:** pain.

Thomas Randolph, 1605–35

In Praise of Women in General: from *Poems, with the Muses' Looking-Glass and Amyntas,* 2nd edn (1640). **8 you . . . earth:** Genesis 2. **10 seed:** Christ. **11–12 Adam . . . rib:** Genesis 2:21–2. **21 Parians:** Paros was celebrated for its white marble. **23 quickness:** liveliness. **25 fronts:** foreheads. **36 tree:** of knowledge of good and evil (Genesis 2:17, 3:6). **40 Samson:** yielded to Delilah (Judges 16); **David** to Uriah's wife, Bathsheba (II Samuel 11). **56 tub:** the Cynic philosopher Diogenes (fifth century BC) reputedly lived in a tub as a mark of austerity.

Anne Bradstreet, 1612–72

From **The Four Ages of Man (Childhood):** from *The Tenth Muse Lately Sprung up in America* (1650). **1 conceived in sin:** Psalm 51:5; **born in sorrow:** Genesis 3:16.

Before the Birth of One of Her Children: from *Several Poems* (1678). **13 days . . . due:** 70 years (Psalm 90:10). **16 oblivious:** forgotten; encouraging forgetfulness. **26 hearse:** coffin.

Henry Vaughan, 1621–95

The Tempest, ll. 5–16:   from *Silex Scintillans* (1655).

Katherine Philips, 1632–64

Epitaph: On Her Son H.P., at St Syth's Church, Where Her Body Also Lies Interred: in *Poems by Mrs Katherine Philips, the Matchless Orinda* (1667). **Title:** St Syth's: St Benet's Sherehog in Syth's Lane. **16 Hermes'-seal:** airtight seal.

Thomas Creech, translator, 1659–1700

[Mother Venus]:   from *Titus Lucretius Carus, His Six Books of Epicurean Philosophy, Done into English Verse* by Thomas Creech (1683), Book I, ll. 1–34. Text, 4th edn (1699). **1 Kind:** natural, benevolent (translating Lucretius' *alma* = nourishing). **10 gaudy:** splendid, joyful. **21 Favonius:** the benign westerly spring wind.

Ambrose Philips, 1674–1749

To Miss Charlotte Pulteney in Her Mother's Arms, 1 May 1724:   from *Poems* (1725). **16 linlet:** baby linnet.

Mary Barber, c. 1690–1757

Written for My Son, and Spoken by Him at His First Putting on Breeches: from *The Flower-Piece: A Collection of Miscellany Poems*, ed. M. Concanen (1731). **Title:** boys wore frocks for the first few years of life. The Son is Constantine Barber (c. 1713–83). **5 ligation:** binding. **27 date:** life.

Mehetabel Wright, 1697–1750

To an Infant Expiring the Second Day of its Birth: from the *Gentleman's Magazine*, October 1733.

Elizabeth Boyd, fl. 1727–45

On the Death of an Infant of Five Days Old, Being a Beautiful but Abortive Birth: from *The Humorous Miscellany: Or, Riddles for the Beaux* (1733).

William Cowper, 1731–1800

On the Receipt of My Mother's Picture Out of Norfolk, The Gift of My Cousin Ann Bodham: from *Poems* (1798). **19 Elysian:** i.e., that he is wandering in Elysium (the fields of the blessed dead of ancient Graeco-Roman belief). **61 confectionary:** crystallised or sugared. **66 brakes:** briers, thickets. **76 jessamine:** jasmine. **97 'Where ... roar':** Samuel Garth, *The Dispensary* (1699), canto IV, lines 225–6 ('To die is landing on some silent shore,/Where billows never break, nor tempests roar'). **109 From ... earth:** Cowper's mother was descended from Henry III.

Anne Hunter, 1742–1821

A Pastoral Song: from *Poems* (1802).

Anna Laetitia Barbauld, 1743–1825

Washing Day, ll. 46–86:   from the *Monthly Magazine*, 4 (1797). **37 Montgolfier:** the first flights in hot-air balloons were made by the Montgolfier brothers in 1783.

To a Little Invisible Being Who is Expected Soon to Become Visible: from *Works* (1825). **2 moon:** here, as at **24**, not merely a poeticism for month, but a reminder of Lucina, the moon goddess who protects mothers giving birth. **5 curious:** ingeniously wrought. **9 genial:** encouraging growth (and thereby invoking Genius, the god of generation); mild. **12 blow:** bloom. **35 bid my beads:** pray my rosary.

Ann Yearsley, 1752–1806

To Mira, On the Care of Her Infant: from *The Rural Lyre* (1796). **10 spray:** branch.

Jane Cave, c. 1754–1813

An Elegy on a Maiden Name: from *Poems on Various Subjects* (2nd edn, 1786). The poem refers to her marriage to Mr Winscomb between 1783 (the date of the publication of the first edition of her *Poems*) and the date of the second edition. **21 helpmates:** Genesis 2:20 (Eve is created as 'an help meet for [Adam]': the origin of the word helpmate).

Written a Few Hours Before the Birth of a Child: from *Poems on Various Subjects* (2nd edn, 1786).

Hannah Wallis, fl. 1787

The Female's Lamentations; or, The Village in Mourning: from *The Female's Meditations; Or, Common Occurrences Spiritualised in Verse* (1787). **14 Hall:** Broomfield Hall, in Essex (author's note). **18 His Honour:** the late Hon. Edward Hatton, Esq. (author's note). **58 eye-strings:** the muscles and nerves of the eye, believed to break at the moment of death. **75 dropped . . . dead:** the author's father dropped down dead in Chelmsford market, Essex (author's note). **85 birthday night:** public celebration of a royal birthday.

Helen Leigh, fl. 1788

The Natural Child: from *Miscellaneous Poems* (1788).

William Blake, 1757–1827

The Little Boy Found: from *Songs of Innocence* (1789).

The Land of Dreams: from the Pickering MS (Pierpoint Morgan Library); often reprinted.

Henrietta O'Neill, 1758–93

Written on Seeing Her Two Sons at Play: from Charlotte Smith, *Elegiac Sonnets*, vol. II (1797).

Isabella Kelly, c. 1759–1857

To an Unborn Infant: from *A Collection of Poems and Fables* (1794). **12 unblown:** unopened.

Joanna Baillie, 1762–1851

From **A Winter's Day:** from *Poems* (1790).

A Mother to Her Waking Infant: from *Poems* (1790). **1 dazzling:** dazed (just possibly, bright). **18 silly:** pitiable; weak. **47 sweepy:** sweeping.

Anon, fl. 1798

On My Own Little Daughter, Four Years Old: from *Poems on Various Subjects. By a Lady* (1798).

William Wordsworth, 1770–1850

The Sailor's Mother: from *Poems* (1807).

The Cottager to Her Infant: from *Poems* (1815).

Confirmation Continued: from *Poems* (1827). **9 amain:** forthwith; uncontrollably.

Mary Tighe, 1772–1810

Sonnet Addressed to My Mother: from the Preface to *Psyche; or, the Legend of Love* (1805).

Samuel Taylor Coleridge, 1772–1834

Sonnet: from *Poems* (1828). **1 Charles:** Charles Lamb (1775–1834), whose long friendship with Coleridge began when they were at school together at Christ's Hospital.

A Child's Evening Prayer: written 1808?: first published in *Poems*, ed. Derwent and Sara Coleridge (1852).

'The Singing Kettle and the Purring Cat': from a manuscript notebook of 1803; first published in *Poetical Works*, ed. J.D. Campbell (1893).

Thomas Moore, 1779–1852

To My Mother: from *Poetical Works* (1854). **1 Indian tree:** the banyan, or Indian fig, as in Milton, *Paradise Lost*, IX.1101–1110 ('spreads her arms/Branching so broad and long, that in the ground/The bended twigs take root, and daughters grow/About the mother tree . . .').

Felicia Hemans, 1793–1835

To My Mother: from *Complete Poems* (n.d.). **53 Aeolian lyre:** a wooden box strung with gut strings of various thickness which sounded when the wind (**Aeolus** was the Graeco-Roman wind god) passed over them; a great favourite in the earlier nineteenth century, it was often placed by an open window, and was the Regency equivalent of the now fashionable wind chimes.

Caroline Clive, 1801–73

The Mother: from *Poems by 'V', the Author of 'Paul Ferroll'* (1872). **10**
forfeit . . . race: Genesis 2:17. **42 Thou . . . dust:** 1 Corinthians 15:22.

Charles Swain, 1801–74

A Mother's Love: from *English Melodies* (1849).

The Widowed Mother: from *English Melodies* (1849).

William Barnes, 1801–86

The Mother's Dream: from *Poems of Rural Life in the Dorset Dialect*
(1879).

Winthrop Mackworth Praed, 1802–39

Mater Desiderata: from *Poems* (1885). **Title:** the longed-for mother
(Latin).

Sara Coleridge, 1802–52

The Mother: from *Pretty Lessons in Verse* (1845 edn). **3 amain:** see
Wordsworth, Confirmation Continued, 9n. above.

Thomas Aird, 1802–76

My Mother's Grave: from *Poetical Works* (1878). **94 awful:** command-
ing awe and reverential fear.

Elizabeth Barrett Browning, 1806–61

Aurora Leigh (1857), Book 1   (lines unnumbered).

Isobel's Child, stanzas 1–8: from *Poetical Works* (1866). **32 rose of Harpocrate:** Harpocrates (Greek name for Egyptian Horus), infant god of silence and son of Isis, is depicted seated on a rose or rose-pink lotus.

Alfred, Lord Tennyson, 1809–92

The Grandmother: originally printed in *Once a Week*, 16 July 1859 as 'The Grandmother's Apology', and with the present title in *The Holy Grail and Other Poems* (1870). **28 tongue . . . fire** James 3:6.

Demeter and Persephone (In Enna), ll. 34–86: from *Demeter and Other Poems* (1889). One of the archetypal mother-daughter myths: Persephone, daughter of Demeter and Zeus, was abducted into the underworld by Dis, god of the infernal regions, as she was gathering flowers on the plains of Enna in Sicily. Her grieving mother eventually found out what had happened to her, and Zeus arranged for the girl to be restored to Demeter for half the year. **6 Aidoneus:** Dis. **49 three . . . heads:** the three Fates who between them spin, wind and cut the thread of human life.

'Remembering Him Who Waits Thee Far Away':   first printed in *Alfred Lord Tennyson: A Memoir* (1897) by Hallam Lord Tennyson. Written at the request of Princess Beatrice for the prayer-book given to the Queen by her grandchildren on the fiftieth anniversary of her wedding to Prince Albert, 10 February 1890.

Jean Ingelow, 1820–97

Seven Times Seven: Longing for Home: from *Songs of Seven* in *Poems* (1882 edn).

Frederick Locker-Lampson, 1821–95

A Terrible Infant: from *London Lyrics* (1872).

To My Grandmother: from *Poems* (1883). **Subtitle: Mr Romney:** George Romney (1734–1802), as celebrated in his time as Reynolds and Gainsborough, especially known for his portraits of young people. **14–15** *coquette falbala:* furbelow (or flounce); or a showy trimming for a scarf or petticoat. **16 limning:** painting. **44 bombazine:** a corded or twilled dress material of silk and worsted. **56 fardel:** burden.

Coventry Patmore, 1823–96

The Toys: from the *Pall Mall Gazette*, 30 November 1876.

Charles Stuart Calverley, 1831–84

Waiting: from *Fly Leaves* (1872).

Motherhood: from *Fly Leaves* (1872).

On the Brink: from *Fly Leaves* (1872). **15 Rhadamanthus:** one of the judges in the underworld.

Joseph Skipsey, 1832–1903

'Mother Wept, and Father Sigh'd':   from *Songs and Lyrics* (1892 edn).

Ellen Johnston, 1835–73

A Mother's Love: from *Autobiography, Poems, and Songs* (2nd edn, 1869). **4 Mary Achin:** the baby, Mary Achenvole, was born when her mother was single and seventeen, in September 1852.

Thomas Hardy, 1840–1928

News for Her Mother: from *Time's Laughingstocks and Other Verses* (1909).

The Christening: from *Time's Laughingstocks* (1909).

In Childbed: from *Time's Laughingstocks* (1909).

Alice Meynell, 1847–1922

The Modern Mother: from *Collected Poems* (1913).

Maternity: from *Collected Poems* (1913).

The Girl on the Land: from *Collected Poems* (1913).

Robert Louis Stevenson, 1850–94

To Alison Cunningham From Her Boy: Dedication to *A Child's Garden of Verses* (1885).

To My Mother: Envoy 2 to *A Child's Garden of Verses* (1885).

To Any Reader: Envoy 6 to *A Child's Garden of Verses* (1885).

Edith Nesbit, 1858–1924

Song: from *Lays and Legends* (1886).

Francis Thompson, 1859–1907

'Little Jesus': from *Works* (1913).

John Masefield, 1878–1967

To His Mother, C.L.M.:   from *Collected Poems* (London: Heinemann, 1923).

Lilian Bowes Lyon, 1895–1949

A Son: from *Tomorrow is a Revealing* (London: Jonathan Cape, 1941).

Anon, twentieth century, oral

The Death of Queen Jane: from Mrs Russell, Upwey, Dorset, 1907; collected by H.E.D. Hammond, text from *The Oxford Book of English Traditional Verse*, ed. Frederick Woods (Oxford, New York: Oxford University Press, 1983), p. 18. 1 Queen Jane: Jane Seymour, third wife of Henry VIII, who died giving birth to the future Edward VI on 13 October 1537. 16 flamboys: flambeaux (torches).

Anon, twentieth century, oral

Whistle, Daughter, Whistle: from Walter Locock, Marton, Somerset, 1906; collected by Cecil Sharp; text from Woods, as above, pp. 61–2.

Anon, twentieth century, oral

The Cruel Mother: from Mrs Bowring, Cerne Abbas, Dorset, 1907; collected by H.E.D. Hammond; text from Woods, as above, pp. 202–3.

Anon, twentieth century, oral

'Where Have You Been All Day':   from Mrs Holden, Worcestershire, 1960s; collected by Fred Hamer; text from Woods, as above, p. 203.

Anon, twentieth century, oral

'All Under the Leaves':   from Mrs Whatton and Mrs Loveridge, Dilwyn, Herefordshire, 1908; collected by Ralph Vaughan Williams; text from Woods, as above, p. 226. **29 John:** see **Anon, fifteenth century, 'Mary Mother, Come and See'**, 21–2n. above.

Anne Ridler, b. 1912

For a Child Expected: from *The Nine Bright Shiners* (London: Faber and Faber, 1943). **31–2 as the sun . . . was:** quoted from the Christmas carol 'In Bethlehem that fair city'; the carol exists in several versions, and the quotation seems to be from the one found in Trinity College, Cambridge, MS 0.3.58, stanza 3 of which begins: 'As sun shineth through the glass,/ So Jesu in his mother was . . .' (R.L. Greene, *The Early English Carols* (Oxford: Clarendon Press, 1935), p. 15).

George Barker, 1913–91

To My Mother: first published in *Eros and Dogma* (1944); text from *Collected Poems* (London: Faber and Faber, 1957). **5 Rabelais:** François Rabelais (c. 1494–c. 1553), erudite French humanist and physician, most familiar for his bawdy, witty and virtuoso five-volume prose satire known collectively as *Gargantua and Pantagruel* (1532–64).

Elizabeth Jennings, b. 1926

To My Mother at 73:   from *Consequently I Rejoice* (Manchester: Carcanet, 1977).

Acknowledgements

The editor and publisher would like to thank the following for permission to reproduce copyright, archive and library material:

The Masters and Fellows of Balliol College, Oxford for Anon, 'What, Heard Ye Not?' MS 354; The Bodleian Library, University of Oxford, for John Audelay, 'The Mother of Mary', MS Douce 302, fol. 31r-v; The British Library for Anon, 'Noel, el, el, el, el, el, ...' and Anon, 'Mary Mother, Come and See', MS Sloane 2593; The Syndics of Cambridge University Library for James Ryman, 'Meekly We Sing Say to Thee', MS Ee. 1.12.; Carcanet Press Limited for Anne Ridler, 'For a Child Expected' from *Collected Poems*, Carcanet (1977); Faber and Faber Ltd for George Barker, 'To My Mother' from *Collected Poems* (1957); David Higham Associates on behalf of the author for Elizabeth Jennings, 'To My Mother at 73' from *Consequently I Rejoice*, Carcanet (1977); Random House Group Ltd for Lilian Bowes Lyon, 'A Son' from *Tomorrow is a Revealing*, Jonathan Cape (1941); The Society of Authors as the Literary Representative of the Estate of the author for John Masefield, 'To His Mother, CLM' from *Collected Poems* (1923);

Every effort has been made to trace all the copyright holders, but if any have been inadvertently overlooked the publishers will be pleased to make the necessary arrangement at the first opportunity.